Prai

Relei

"I've known Luis Miranda as a
political warrior and social activi
lines of so many important battles.
great storyteller!"

"From the streets of Puerto Rico t
York City, Luis Miranda has lived
on building community and lifting
mination and eclectic influences (
make him one of the most fascina
Relentless introduces you to an exempl
story—regardless of political leanings–
—Gove

"Who on earth would include a thoroug
in his autobiography? Only someone
visionary, as Luis Miranda! In this book
path to living life to the fullest, building
creating positive change, celebrating La
looking poignantly toward the future. A
who enjoys fast-paced, tongue-in-cheek,
dictable storytelling, that at times is laugh
charming, deeply compelling, and powerfu

Relentless

My Story of the Latino Spirit
That Is Transforming America

LUIS A. MIRANDA JR.
WITH RICHARD WOLFFE

hachette
BOOKS

New York

Copyright © 2024 by Luis A. Miranda Jr.

Cover design by Amanda Kain
Cover photograph by John James
Cover copyright © 2024 by Hachette Book Group, Inc.

Hachette Book Group supports the right to free expression and the value of copyright. The purpose of copyright is to encourage writers and artists to produce the creative works that enrich our culture.

The scanning, uploading, and distribution of this book without permission is a theft of the author's intellectual property. If you would like permission to use material from the book (other than for review purposes), please contact Permissions@hbgusa.com. Thank you for your support of the author's rights.

Hachette Books
Hachette Book Group
1290 Avenue of the Americas
New York, NY 10104
HachetteBooks.com
Twitter.com/HachetteBooks
Instagram.com/HachetteBooks

First Edition: May 2024

Published by Hachette Books, an imprint of Hachette Book Group, Inc. The Hachette Books name and logo are trademarks of the Hachette Book Group.

The Hachette Speakers Bureau provides a wide range of authors for speaking events. To find out more, visit hachettespeakersbureau.com or email HachetteSpeakers@hbgusa.com.

Books by Hachette Books may be purchased in bulk for business, educational, or promotional use. For information, please contact your local bookseller or email the Hachette Book Group Special Markets Department at Special.Markets@hbgusa.com.

The publisher is not responsible for websites (or their content) that are not owned by the publisher.

Print book interior design by Amy Quinn

Library of Congress Cataloging-in-Publication Data

Names: Miranda, Luis A., author. | Wolffe, Richard, 1968– author.
Title: Relentless: my story of the Latino spirit that is transforming
    America / Luis A. Miranda, Jr.; with Richard Wolffe.
Description: First edition. | New York, NY: Hachette Books, 2024. | Includes index.
Identifiers: LCCN 2023041342 | ISBN 9780306833229 (hardcover) |
    ISBN 9780306833236 (trade paperback) | ISBN 9780306833243 (ebook)
Subjects: LCSH: Miranda, Luis A. | Puerto Ricans—New York (State)—New
    York—Biography. | Political consultants—New York (State)—New York—Biography. |
    New York (N.Y.)—Biography. | Puerto Rico—Biography.
Classification: LCC F128.57.M57 A3 2024 | DDC 974.7/10046872950092
    [B]—dc23/eng/20240117
LC record available at https://lccn.loc.gov/2023041342

ISBNs: 978-0-306-83322-9 (hardcover), 978-0-306-83324-3 (ebook),
978-0-306-83556-8 (Spanish-language paperback), 978-0-306-83557-5
(Spanish-language ebook)

Printed in the United States of America

LSC-H

Printing 1, 2024

To all of those in Puerto Rico who nurtured me, loved me, and carried me for the first nineteen years of my life, and to the many in New York and everywhere who supported me, guided me, and gave me more love for the last fifty.

Contents

Contents

Foreword

by Lin-Manuel Miranda

I AM THE MOST LAID-BACK MEMBER OF MY FAMILY.

I tell this to reporters, and their faces become emojis of surprise. "You? Mr. Six-Years-Writing-the-20,520-Word-*Hamilton*? Mr. Every-Other-Disney-Soundtrack? Mr. 'Maaan, the Man Is Nonstop'?"

To which I reply, "Yes. I am the family slacker. You should meet my dad."

And if they are lucky enough to meet Luis A. Miranda Jr., they return to me with a face of shock and not a little sympathy: "Oh, Lin. You weren't kidding."

If you're reading this book, you're about to understand.

———

IN HIS TYPICAL OVERACHIEVING FASHION, LUIS HAS REALLY written three books. There is his life story, as improbable as that of his favorite character, Debbie Reynolds's *Unsinkable Molly Brown*, in which he journeys from the small town of Vega Alta, Puerto Rico, to find love, a family, and a true home in New York City. The second book is a gripping firsthand account of the growing political power of Latinos in New York City in the latter half of the twentieth century as disparate communities from Puerto Rico, the Dominican Republic, Mexico, and Latin America found common cause in coalition with their neighbors and power in unity. From there emerges a third book, an indispensable political handbook on the "Latino voter," that most prized and mysterious growing electorate, a favorite topic of political pundits everywhere. Luis debunks, interrogates, and separates fact from fiction with the authority of over forty-five years of political experience.

If you're a political junkie whose diet consists of any amounts of MSNBC, CNN, FOX, PBS, NPR, the *New York Times*, the *Washington Post*, the *Wall Street Journal*, or any combination thereof, this third book is excellent reading.

If you're a history buff who loves to read about how power and people and movements shape cities and vice versa—i.e., if you've got a Robert Caro book somewhere on your shelf—this second book is indispensable reading.

Then there is that first book, the story of Luis Miranda's extraordinary and improbable life. The life that, thanks to a chance meeting with a prospective graduate student named Luz Elaine Towns at NYU in 1976, is responsible for my existence.

I have no objectivity when it comes to this first book.

If your father wrote about the many years before you and the many years after you, what would you learn?

I learned *a lot*.

That a man named Bernie Kalinkowitz quietly revolutionized student recruiting and, in offering my Puerto Rican father admission to college in New York, changed the trajectory of all our lives forever.

That decades before I began creating theater, my great-uncle Ernesto Concepción was performing to acclaim on stages all over Puerto Rico, instilling in my father a love of theater that would take root and blossom most unexpectedly a generation later.

That my grandfather was even more of a saint than I already thought he was.

That my mother makes a mean lobster dinner, but it comes with a side dish of humility.

That the Irish American exodus from Upper Manhattan is directly responsible for our childhood home.

That my father skipped first grade—through sheer force of will.

It also confirms something that I've always known on a cellular level: that my father's work is the all-time great love of his life. His work, his life's work, is making life better for Latinos in this country. He is consumed with getting as much done in this one precious life as time will allow. He wakes up thinking about how he can be more effective at getting something done and, once he's accomplished the task at hand, how much more he can take on.

When you're young, that can be a tough lesson to absorb, even unconsciously: though you may be the main character in your own story, you are not the center of your parent's universe. And yet Luis also manages to be a fierce, loyal friend, a supportive father (never missed a school play, even while juggling multiple jobs), and a doting grandfather in his spare time: all part of his life's work.

In his work making life better for others, he taught me empathy and humility for the larger human collective. In our trips to Puerto Rico, he connected my sister and me to our greater ancestry. In the pursuit of his dreams, Luis modeled for me how to fall in love with my work and chase dreams of my own.

Reading this book makes me want to work harder. Even as the most laid-back Miranda in the family.

You're about to understand.

Siempre,
Lin-Manuel Miranda

CHAPTER 1

Arrival

I LANDED AT JFK WITH A SINGLE PIECE OF LUGGAGE: A BIG GREEN trunk full of books that defined my tastes—from psychology to revolutionary Latin America and colonial Puerto Rico. It was Labor Day weekend of 1974, and I had just turned twenty. Behind me in Puerto Rico was all I had known of home: my young wife, my beautiful apartment, my car, my job at Sears, my plans to study law, my family, my political activism. The enduring heat of summer in the Caribbean gave way to the cooler weather of the East Coast. On the TWA plane, one sentimental song drifted through my head on a loop: "The Way We Were," from a Barbra Streisand and Robert Redford film about a Marxist activist, wasted talent, and doomed young romance. Within a year I would be divorced from my seventh grade sweetheart, but for now I was in denial and looking ahead.

Meeting me at the airport was my New York aunt, Myrta, and her date of the week, driving his small two-door car. She took one look at the big trunk. "You didn't say you were bringing that fucking thing," she said in despair. I squeezed into the back seat, with the heavy trunk half balanced on my lap, as we made our way into Manhattan. It was a clear, sunny day, and when we drove by St. Michael's Cemetery in Queens, I was astonished by its sheer size. "Everyone is dead here," I blurted out as we passed a small town of tombstones. There was no place in Puerto Rico where there were so many dead people. A few minutes later, the city skyline rose up before me. My eyes were drawn to the majestic view of the Empire State and Chrysler buildings. The greatness of this city, its life and its spirit, were clear well before we reached our destination: 234 West Twenty-First Street in Chelsea.

The neighborhood felt overwhelmingly Puerto Rican, especially where my aunt lived. In the basement, there was a billiard table and dominoes for people to play and hang out. It was packed well into the night, with people arriving just to have a great time underneath an apartment building. The area was beginning to change—to gentrify with more white, more wealthy newcomers—but for now it was a vibrant mix of my old life and what lay ahead.

I had arranged to meet some friends that first night, at 10:00 p.m., including several new arrivals from Puerto Rico. "What's your address?" asked my friend Ismael. "I don't know, but it's on Twenty-First Street past Seventh Avenue," I told him. "There's a fire escape in front of the building." He finally called me, exasperated, from a pay phone in the street. "Luisito, do you understand that every building on Twenty-First Street has a fire escape?"

I was clueless but would learn quickly. My friends helped me reset my expectations and understanding of our place in this city: of who we were and what we could become. Among them was Nydia Velázquez, born in Yabucoa and now studying at New York University, where I was headed myself. Two decades later, Nydia would become the first Puerto Rican woman elected to the US Congress. But on this incredible September night, she was one more reason why I knew I had made the right decision. The assumption back home was that the Puerto Ricans who left for New York—the Nuyoricans—were the huddled masses, the poor and uneducated, journeying to do the manual work others wouldn't. But here I was meeting up at a coffeehouse with friends from Puerto Rico and other Latinos, born and raised in New York, studying political science and psychology, and there was nothing uneducated about them. They were cool, and I was in awe of their ambition and drive to succeed in a city with so much energy. They were the smartest and most adventurous of our people.

I was even more in awe of a city where there were as many people on the streets at 1:00 a.m., when we finished our coffee, as there had been at 3:00 p.m., when I had arrived from the airport. I returned to my aunt's place, where the television was still on. At midnight back home, the streets were long deserted and there was nothing but static snow on TV. So I stayed up to watch a movie, *Madame X* with Lana Turner. I cried my eyes out at the story of a lower-class woman who marries into money but is left without her husband, her son, and her identity. It doesn't take much for me to lose my distance when I'm watching movies. I could cry watching *Batman*, because movies open the lid of the pent-up sorrow that I carry within me. Sorrow from injustices I see around me or from having left Puerto Rico fifty years ago. In real life, it's much easier for me to get in touch with my anger than my sadness. At the end of a manic day, *Madame X* was an escape valve to feel the loss of what I had left behind and make room for the promise of what lay ahead.

The next morning, I headed to NYU to begin my new life. My aunt gave me her pithy, witty science of New York City geography, based on race. "There is uptown, and there is downtown," she explained. "You know you are going downtown because it gets considerably darker. And when you go uptown, it gets whiter and whiter." She also told me that Fifth Avenue divides the west from the east. And with that knowledge, I was ready to face New York. Fortunately, I could just walk fifteen blocks to Washington Square, the heart of NYU.

New York had not been part of my plans just six months earlier. Back home, I was heading to law school at the University of Puerto Rico to begin what I thought would be a career in politics when another aunt—the acting chair of psychology at UPR—told me that an NYU chair was coming to interview students.

"I'm going to law school," I told her.

"Yeah, but you don't lose anything coming to the interview," she replied.

I didn't know it at the time, but I was about to become part of a radical experiment in racial quotas. The NYU psychology chair, Bernie Kalinkowitz, planned to accept twenty PhD candidates in clinical psychology: ten whites, five Hispanics, and five African Americans. I didn't quite comprehend what was going on because coming from Puerto Rico, I didn't feel disadvantaged. Back home, Puerto Ricans sweep the floors, but we also perform heart transplants. It's the same people doing everything. The notion of ethnic minorities being underprivileged was new to me—not in concept but en carne y hueso, up close. I knew about poverty and the working class versus the ruling class. But the idea that minorities, rather than class, meant something pejorative was unusual for me. I had read plenty about the way Black people were treated in the United States, about the way Mexicans were conquered and the way Native Americans had suffered genocide and been relegated to reservations of land. I could understand it intellectually, but I didn't understand it emotionally. I never felt it in my heart.

My first meeting at NYU was with the student who had recruited me, Jeanette Rossello, who reminded me that I was part of this relatively new policy to diversify the program. Within days, I was at my first meeting of minority students. There I met a young woman named Kamala. She was at NYU as one of the Black recruits, but she looked white to me. It really blew my mind. Alongside me was a Nuyorican friend, Lillian, who was one of the five Latinos. I asked her naively, "Why is Kamala Black?"

"I think her dad was Black and her mother was Hawaiian," she explained. Kamala looked white to me, but because of her father, she was considered Black.

"OK," I said as I tried to reconcile all of these new concepts that I had read about in books but was now struggling to understand. Lillian herself was dating a Black Dominican, while another student in my cohort, Javier, was Dominican. All of a sudden, reality was different from my experience of the first two decades of my life, and I was trying to figure out where I fit in.

Don't get me wrong. Racial lines were real back home: there was Black and white and many skin colors in between. But the actual color of your skin was more important than your ancestry when it came to determining race. In New York City, I was in a whole new world where ancestry was taken into account, and I didn't know the rules of the game that were so important to people in the United States. Back in Puerto Rico, my grandfather on my mother's side was Black with wavy hair, and he married my grandmother, who was blond and blue-eyed. He was the son of more affluent Puerto Ricans. She was sixteen or seventeen when they married, and she was just one of many beautiful poor white girls from the countryside. My mother was white, even though her ancestry was similar to Kamala's. I was learning that race was defined openly, rigidly, and permanently on the mainland.

As if race were not confusing enough, I also had to adapt to becoming a Spanish-speaking immigrant in a country where I was also a citizen. I was sharing a bedroom with my eight-year-old and four-year-old cousins, who were my first English teachers. They would laugh endlessly at my mistakes, correcting me between giggles. But at least I could hear them speak English incessantly, and I could practice it safely. It was a welcoming place to land in the big city. My aunt welcomed everyone into her two-bedroom apartment, but she insisted that her room was hers. "Only my boyfriends sleep with me," she said.

The real impact of immigration hit me hard when another two friends from my town joined us, sleeping in the living room, and my aunt soon had a proposition for one of them. A friend of a friend was looking for someone he could pay to be his wife so he could become a citizen.

"You have to be married for a year," she told them. "You don't have to have sex, but you have to live together."

She sounded like Oprah telling her audience they were getting a car.

"So one of you has got yourself an apartment. Who wants to get married?"

We spent a good amount of time meeting this prospective husband and then collectively deciding who was going to marry him. This was my introduction to the perils of immigration.

When I left the islands, there were a handful of Dominicans and plenty of Cubans there who had come as refugees and soon risen through Puerto Rico's social structures. But there were no minority immigrants to speak of, and there was no widespread scheme of finding fake husbands or wives so they could stay.

New York's Latino community was changing from being Puerto Rican-centric to being much more diverse. The children of Puerto Ricans, along with the hundreds of thousands who had traveled to New York in the late 1940s and 1950s, were becoming part of a truly Hispanic community.

———

I HAD NO IDEA AT THE TIME THAT I WOULD DEDICATE MY PROFES-sional life to navigating this new world of race, ethnicity, class, and immigration. I had no idea that this city would be the perfect place to combine my political instincts and psychological insights to help candidates and elected officials navigate the same world for themselves. And I certainly had no idea that I could help build community—through nonprofits, government, and the arts—to help my new neighbors survive and thrive.

My career has often been shaped by a simple-sounding question: what do Latinos want? It's a question that is being posed more often and more loudly as the demographics and politics of this country progress steadily toward a new future. And it has become central to living in our communities, as Republicans use migrants and Latinos as pawns in their political chess games. The majority of this new country will be a combination of minorities within the next two decades. Much of that change is from the rapid growth of the communities that have been my focus for decades. Several years after I arrived in New York, the 1980 census showed that 80 percent of the population of the country was white, 11 percent was Black, and just 6.5 percent was Latino or Hispanic. Within two decades, Latinos outnumbered Blacks. Today, the white population is 60 percent of the country and falling, while Latinos and Asian Americans represent almost 25 percent of this country. How you feel about these changes has become a defining measure of whether you are conservative or progressive. It's no coincidence that a corrupt New York real estate developer, trained in the racial politics of the 1980s tabloids, could ride a wave of nativist and racist feeling all the way to the White House. A majority of Republicans—59 percent—think this diverse majority will lead to more racial conflict and weaken this country's values and customs. That's why clowns like Governor Ron DeSantis of Florida and Governor Greg Abbott of Texas have created havoc by sending asylum seekers to Democratic cities.

These are not small changes, and the question about Latinos and Latino voters is a valid one. However, in most circles, and certainly in the media, it is fundamentally flawed and wrongly framed. Understanding why can help decision-makers—in politics and in business—answer the question for themselves. Too often Latino political views are seen as being in the middle, somewhere between whites and Blacks. We end up as the average of multiple measured variables.

In fact, let me be provocative: there is no such thing as a Hispanic voting bloc. Although we have much in common, communities that make up this group are as varied in background, class, and race as the entire hemisphere. There's a huge diversity of Latinos in the United States today. We are no longer just Mexicans, or Puerto Ricans who started arriving in the 1950s, or Cubans who came in the 1960s. Over the last several years, we have seen new waves of Latino immigrants trying to create a new life in a country that's in a different place every time a new wave arrives. The desire to consider them a single voting bloc comes from the brutal and rigid legacy of slavery and Jim Crow that intentionally erased the different identities of African Americans. Their shared generational suffering has created patterns of politics that can be generalized to seem more predictable. There is nothing equivalent in the Latino or Hispanic experience, and assuming that some parallel exists does not make it so.

It's not just voters with family ties to Cuba; there are now Venezuelans who came here for the same reasons as Cuban families, with similar political attitudes as they seek asylum. They are arriving at a time when the Democratic Party is in a battle between the left, the center, and the right. While Republicans are a monolithic party, aligned with Trump and engaged in the culture wars, Democrats have a diversity of opinions and messengers. Some of those messengers are not ideal for some Latino communities. Ten seconds of Bernie Sanders, a huge figure in the Democratic Party, talking nicely about Fidel Castro becomes the headline.

"We're very opposed to the authoritarian nature of Cuba, but you know, it's unfair to simply say everything is bad," Bernie told *60 Minutes* on CBS. "When Fidel Castro came into office, you know what he did? He had a massive literacy program. Is that a bad thing? Even though Fidel Castro did it?"

As Joe Biden was trying to unify the party so that Democrats could win, Sanders offered an opportunity for Republicans to say, "You see, they're married. The guy who thinks Fidel Castro is the best thing since sliced bread is now in bed with the guy who says he's from the center."

Let me make it more complicated: we can also behave as a voting bloc. Our political beliefs are shaped not only by our origin but also by a shared language and our immigrant experience once we are here. Campaigns need to speak about our concerns and our hopes and how we relate to others who were here before us—and that needs to happen in two languages. Candidates and pundits need to know a bit about this audience before they open their mouths, particularly if they don't have a history with the Latino community. Language is a proxy for respect and understanding, for cultural sensitivity and embracing our immigrant experience. Speaking our language appropriately moves Latinos to behave as a voting bloc.

What about those who were born and raised here? English may be their dominant language, but living in multigenerational households exposes many of us to Spanish—whether in our daily routines or through the media. The home I would make in New York would include an English-dominant mom, a Spanish-dominant dad, a Spanish-monolingual "grandma," and three kids born in New York. Communicating in Spanish as well as English in a political campaign shows respect and opens multiple doors to talk to everyone in my household.

That's also true for the one-quarter of the Latino community who are Donald Trump admirers or supporters. When he speaks about race and immigrants, even his Latino fans can frown. But they like him because he's decisive and entertaining. He presents an aura of being in charge. He becomes the symbol of what many of us had in mind when we migrated: be successful! His Latino supporters can disapprove of him demonizing immigrants, or saying that Mexicans are rapists, and still admire him because they aspire to share in an American dream of wealth. When he talks about providing honest work instead of a government handout, many Latinos listen. For many immigrants, governments are not honest and well intentioned. Some Latinos are invested in what Trump represents because they have come from countries that were ruined by corrupt dictators. For those fleeing socialism, when they hear that Democrats are socialists, their life experience or their fears take over. I warned my Democratic friends that we were losing ground in Florida in 2020 because the other side was portraying centrist Joe Biden as a socialist—pointing to Bernie Sanders as his proxy. We believe in the saying "Dime con quien andas, y te diré quien eres." Your friends tell us a lot about who you are.

Campaigns need to make sure their arguments fit the bill. Latinos are increasingly getting their news through Facebook, YouTube, and WhatsApp, and misinformation inundates our brains. Half of the knowledge base upon which we make our political assumptions is not true. You don't go to south Texas and talk about open borders. You go to south Texas to figure out how we have a continued relationship with our southern neighbors and how our new neighbors can come to this country in an orderly fashion. We are building a better country that is a more diverse country, so candidates need to arm their supporters with their best arguments and get them out to vote. Latinos need to be reassured of the truth—that our hopes and dreams will be advanced by good government as well as personal entrepreneurship. The struggles of working people are the same whether you are white, Black, or Brown: to get ahead, to give your kids a better future, to pay medical bills or buy a car. Political leaders need to speak to those struggles—to show the path forward—and deliver on their promises. Republicans do not need a majority of Latino voters to win elections; they just need to peel away enough votes to deny a majority to Democrats. Fear and propaganda can do that, and the only cure is a conversation with trustworthy people who show up in our Latino community. A conversation that moves the world forward, that shows that our leaders know how voters want to move forward. That's what we mean in Puerto Rico when we say pa'lante: it's the drive to keep moving ahead, to build a better future.

———

MY PURPOSE IN LIFE WAS POLITICAL, AND I SOUGHT OUT LIKE-minded souls in New York. The first thing I did on arriving in New York was ask my friends whether there was a movement here. They knew what I meant. We had been part of the student movement to democratize the University of Puerto Rico, and they put me in contact with other "independentistas" who had come to New York. A couple of weeks later, I was selling *Claridad*, the Puerto Rican Socialist Party's newspaper, on the Lower East Side. It was there, on what we called Loisaida, that I met "independentistas" who had been born in New York as well as those born on the archipelago.

I quickly understood that the movement was divided between those who thought our main goal was to fight for Puerto Rican independence from the United States and those who thought the Puerto Ricans who left had to join other minorities to fight for the civil and democratic rights of Puerto Ricans and other oppressed groups living on the mainland. In retrospect, I have to wonder why we couldn't do both. But at the time, this was fundamental to our identity. Were we an extension of the Puerto Rican nation or an oppressed national minority, like Native Americans, Black Americans, and other immigrants? Were we fighting for the rights of Puerto Rico or fighting hand in hand with other minorities for social justice on the mainland? This was just a month after Nixon's resignation as president, but Democrats and Republicans were not my concern. I spent countless hours of twenty-year-old intellect and energy debating these Puerto Rican issues in small rooms in the South Bronx, East Harlem, and Loisaida, where we would go on forever, arguing back and forth.

The real world of politics around me was even more dramatic than Watergate. I arrived in New York just a few years after the Young Lords staged their daring takeovers and occupations, setting up community programs as they advocated for the liberation of Puerto Rico and an end to political and economic oppression in the United States. They were the Puerto Rican offshoot of the Black Panthers, inspired by the student movements of the 1960s as well as the leadership of Huey Newton, Bobby Seale, and Fred Hampton. They took over abandoned buildings to offer free breakfast to children and education to the community. And, following Hampton's assassination in 1969, they knew that the police and FBI were more than ready to shoot them all dead. Their greatest moment in New York was the audacious takeover of Lincoln Hospital in the South Bronx, a local institution with such a dismal record that it was known as the Butcher Shop. On July 14, 1970, a group of 150 Young Lords spent twelve hours inside the decaying building, demanding the construction of a new hospital and free health care. As police prepared to storm the hospital, the Young Lords melted away into the crowd of hospital staff and doctors, with no violence. They emerged with one of the first patient's bills of rights in the country. The hospital would be demolished and rebuilt six years later.

Although the group was not as active when I arrived, I spent many nights hearing their war stories at our weekly political education sessions. It was incredibly rewarding for me to meet leaders like Juan González, who was born in Puerto Rico and founded the New York branch of the Young Lords. They had seen the oppression of their immigrant parents and grandparents in the United States, and their response was direct and refreshing. They were fighting for the democratic rights of an oppressed minority—for proper health care and decent housing. Those would eventually become my goals too. It just took me several years to get there.

Even as the Young Lords became tales of the past, our cause was gaining new energy and attention. One month after I arrived, in October 1974, five large bombs were detonated across Manhattan: two at Rockefeller Center, one in the Financial District, and another two on Park Avenue north of the Waldorf-Astoria. Nobody was injured, but there was extensive property damage. Las Fuerzas Armadas de Liberación Nacional (FALN), or the Armed Forces of National Liberation, claimed responsibility. They demanded independence for Puerto Rico and were more than ready to use violence to meet their ends. Over the next year, they launched a series of attacks, including one that killed four people at Fraunces Tavern near Wall Street, and one day of simultaneous bombings in nine cities that fortunately left nobody hurt.

I was all in favor of independence for Puerto Rico: we were one people, one nation, and it was our job to be inside the belly of the beast, making sure that Puerto Rico became independent. Yet I openly opposed the killing of innocent people. Believe me, that was not a popular position in the movement. However, I was never interested in winning popularity contests. That's one of the reasons I never ran for office. I had learned in my US history classes that the country had gained independence through armed struggle, but I believe that today, a country can become independent without shedding blood. I was never tempted to join a terrorist group or engage in violent action. I had spent my life reading, arguing, and debating. In fact, before I boarded the flight to New York, I had envisioned my life as a lawyer in the world of politics in Puerto Rico.

Soon after the Fraunces Tavern bombing, I went to a pro-independence, pro–Black Panther rally at Madison Square Garden. My aunt told me it wasn't a good idea so soon after the terrorist attack, but in the end, she joined me at the rally. I don't know if she came because she wanted to protect me or because I had convinced her that she really needed to fight, if not for independence, at least for a better life for her children. Either way, the Garden was full of people. The only real debate in my mind was whether an independent Puerto Rico would be capitalist or socialist. I felt that an independent Puerto Rico that simply replaced one ruling class with another was not attractive.

I wanted to make sure that people who didn't have a voice or a future could move forward to a better life.

CHAPTER 2

Origins

I WAS NAMED AFTER MY DAD: LUIS ANTONIO MIRANDA JR. I DID not like being a junior. That's why I always said that when I had a son, his name would not be Luis. My father was a beloved figure where I grew up, in the small town of Vega Alta in northern Puerto Rico. He was good at everything: sports, math, problem-solving. It was tough to be like him, not least because I looked a lot like him: big nose, fair complexion, dark hair. He was a pleasant, handsome guy, probably not more than five foot seven. I promised myself that I wouldn't burden my child with the expectations of being like someone else.

Unlike my father, I sucked at sports, especially baseball. But my dad was big on baseball, first as a lefty pitcher and then in every other position with Los Maceteros de Vega Alta, our local team. He loved nothing more than traveling Puerto Rico as the team played in different towns. When I was growing up, I went to every game. I couldn't hit a ball, but I was great at the theoretical under-pinnings. I kept score by hand and could figure out the batting averages of all the team members in my head. We had no computers or calculators. My younger brother was a baseball player, and years later, he would bring a very different happiness to my dad's life as a Pentecostal minister. But I kept score and was good at theory. I knew when it was a good idea to change the pitcher because I knew everybody's averages. I suppose I was a sabermetrician before that's what they were called.

To distinguish me from my father, everyone called me Luisito: little Luis. To this day, if someone calls me Luisito as I'm walking down the streets of New York, I know they are from my hometown.

Today, my wife, Luz, calls me Luisito only when she wants to make fun of me: "Luisito, do you want me to bring you food?" I was the first grandchild on both sides of my family, so life was a little easier for me. I didn't need to do house chores. I don't remember ever serving myself food. I would just sit down, and food would magically appear. Until I moved to New York as a graduate student, I don't remember ever having to do laundry or figure out how shirts were starched.

Once, in the early days of our marriage, Luz prepared lobsters for dinner. She slapped this crustacean on a plate in front of me, much to my surprise.

"What am I supposed to do with this?"

"You eat it," she said.

"Luz, I don't even know what to do with this. My mother gave me the meat on a plate. You're plopping this horrible monster in front of me."

"Starting today, you won't be un inútil," she said with a big smile.

She was right. Now I cook, wash clothes, starch shirts—and even dismember lobsters.

———

IN PUERTO RICO, I WAS THE GOLDEN CHILD. BUT THAT DOESN'T mean my life was carefree. People expected things of me, and I quickly learned to expect them of myself. While my dad just wanted us to be happy and let us be, my mom and her family had very high expectations. Getting a B in school was really failure for her. The second-best grade was a failure. So I could only get As at school, and I graduated as one of only two kids with a 4.0 average. I always worked hard to get the top grade. I knew there were kids who could show up to class without studying for a test, but I was not one of them. My mother would give me shit if I ever dared to get a B. But my father would ask her to stop: "Ave Maria, Evi, please. He did well." That did not change my mother's mind—or, in fact, my own. She wanted to know what happened, what went wrong. I could explain that nobody got an A on this particular test, so B was the highest grade. But she would insist that I probably hadn't tried hard enough, that I needed to try harder.

My mother didn't expect me to do well; she expected me to be the best. My father, for his part, understood success in completely different ways. For him, success was achieved when you did your best, no matter how you stacked up with others. He was totally happy if I came back from school, played Ping-Pong for three hours, and then did my homework. But my mother wanted me to do the homework first.

She came from a prestigious family on the archipelago. They did not have money, but they had a name: Concepción de Gracia. Her uncle was the founder of the Puerto Rican Independence Party. Her other uncle was a senator representing another party. My mother was Eva Concepción, and she was rightly proud of it.

My dad's family was known locally. My great-aunt (whom I knew as my grandmother since she had raised my dad) was an entrepreneur with a local business and various rental properties. My grandfather was a teacher and civic leader in town. One of his accomplishments was the creation of the town's credit union, which years later my dad would manage. The house where I grew up was my mother's family home, which we took over when her nuclear family moved to San Juan.

My mother was very pretty, with a very fair complexion and long, dark, wavy hair. She was not the mushy type. If you wanted love, you went to her mother, my grandmother Mamá Justa. My mother took care of business: quite literally, she ran her own business. For a long time, a travel agency. Before that, a beauty parlor. She was very practical about life. One day, my father got very angry and threw a plate against the wall. We were all sitting at the table, wondering what would happen next. My mother just looked at him and said, "Now you have to clean it." She continued eating, with no drama.

Every Sunday, we would get in the family car and drive an hour and a half to San Juan to see Mamá Justa and the rest of my mother's family. We would leave Vega Alta early in the morning and have lunch with the family, and then my father and I would go to the movies. Sometimes we would see something we both liked. But other times, he would drop me off at a movie, see something else, and wait for me outside. That was how I ended up watching

The Sound of Music at least eighty times. *The Sound of Music* was always longer than whatever John Wayne movie he wanted to see.

As soon as I was old enough, I would travel on my own to stay at Mamá Justa's in San Juan so I could go to the movies and the theater. On Friday nights, right after school, I would hop in a carro público—a small car for six people—then jump in a minivan in Bayamón, and finally take a bus to my grandparents' home in Country Club, their development in San Juan. My uncle Ernesto was involved in theater, and I loved that life. Early in his educational career, Ernesto recruited me to be in a play he was directing at the University of Puerto Rico. My dad—or someone else from my town—would drive me in the afternoons, after school, to rehearsals. So when my son Lin-Manuel succeeded in theater, his career continued to feed my love of this art form that began at an early age.

My life in San Juan revolved around the movies and theater, and that meant a life of stories and performances. My uncle Rodolfo loved movies and music. He was studying medicine, but during those weekends in San Juan, we would watch movies and listen to music. We would also go to small venues in old San Juan, where there were theater bars. My uncle Ernesto owned one such bar in old San Juan, La Tierruca, where there was poetry and theater, and the family managed it. During my senior year of high school, I loved to work behind the bar, serving drinks and soaking up the culture. Sylvia del Villard performed there, with her groundbreaking shows about Afro-Caribbean culture. When nobody else was talking about the influence of African culture in Puerto Rico, Sylvia was mixing theater, poetry, and dance to tell her story of our country. I was just fifteen, working for free behind the bar, while my grandmother cooked for the customers. We would stay until three or four in the morning, immersed in this creative community.

During my weekends in San Juan, I met the great Walter Mercado, who was an actor and dancer. Mercado grew up in the theater with my uncle, but he later became wildly famous as an astrologer on television, dressed in capes and flamboyant costumes. He was a fascinating character who would read your palm and give you the story told in your cards.

This culture was like another education for me, where I learned that it was normal to embrace different kinds of people: trans kids, gay couples, people with different shades of skin. Today's culture wars, led by racist Republicans, are completely foreign to me because I grew up accepting diversity.

In my last year in high school, I entered a national competition for theater in the category of monologues. I won the prize for the best monologue in the country, and I still have the award in my office at home. It's my favorite award ever! For a brief moment, I wanted to be an actor. But I saw how difficult life was for my uncle Ernesto and how much grief he got from the rest of the family. He wanted to make it as an actor in a country where theater wasn't valued. He was a serious actor who rose to be the president of the Actors Association, and he was fantastic in the business. But he always had numerous jobs because he also had to support his family. His wife was also a great actress, but she gave up her acting career to be a drama teacher, and the pressure on him to do the same was relentless.

I loved this world, but I did not want to struggle like him or deal with the criticism that he endured for his whole life. If I did something, I needed to be successful. That's why I never played music. I do not like to do things by halves, and I never had the discipline to dedicate the time to an instrument. My dad used to say, "You could do things for fun. You don't have to become a classical pianist or guitar player." But I never knew what that meant. Being good enough was not attractive to me. I had to be the best, and I already knew that I would not be excellent. I did not want to be able to just play a song.

When I went to the University of Puerto Rico in San Juan, I lived with my grandmother Mamá Justa. I would sit and talk to her for hours. Her story was inspiring and heartbreaking. She came from a very poor family and lived—in my opinion—like the servant of the family she married into, in the home of her mother-in-law—my great-grandmother, Doña Carmen de Gracia. The whole extended family, husbands, wives, and children, lived there in her big house in San Juan. Mamá Justa told me how everyone's paycheck would go to Doña Carmen, and she would decide what everyone got back. She was determined to ensure that her children were well educated. She was the one who decided to send my uncle, the founder of the Puerto Rican Independence Party, to study law at Georgetown. She decided that my grandfather, the oldest son, would study education. And she insisted that all her daughters would become teachers, because she thought they should not live at the mercy of a man. So while her daughters went to school, my grandmother stayed in the house, washed the clothes, and cooked for them all. She was Cinderella. Her job was to serve others. When she told me these stories, I would be outraged. But she would calm me down by saying, "Everyone has a role to play in life. I was very happy when they graduated. We were all so happy. I was part of that. I did their clothes. I did what I had to do to make that family a success."

"Mamá Justa," I said, "you were the slave for all those entitled kids."

"No," she insisted. "They were wonderful people, and I did my part."

Many years later, I shared this story with the creative team responsible for developing Disney's *Encanto*. Lin-Manuel had been hired to write the story's music and songs, and I became a consultant on the movie. My grandmother's tale became part of the creative team's research on Latin America's reliance on extended family and is a small part of Abuela Madrigal's creative DNA.

I like to think that my first memories are of family. But that's a bit misleading because in the small town where I grew up, everyone is family. My mother spent most of her days at her small travel agency in the middle of Vega Alta. Even at the end of her life, when the internet was slowly killing travel agencies, she spent her time working there. She was in the middle of the action and knew everybody's business in town. It was a tiny space, but lots of people would stop by just to chat.

My parents were intertwined in the civic fiber of the town: in the Lions, the Rotary Club, the Red Cross, the church. And, of course, they were involved in politics. My mother was pro-independence but was quiet about it. For a while, my father supported the Popular Democratic Party (PPD), which advocated for self-governance for Puerto Rico as a commonwealth of the United States, under Luis Muñoz Marín. Politics were so important in our house that one of my favorite games as a kid was to create toy car caravans, with each car carrying little political flags that I had drawn. Over time, my father grew disillusioned with the PPD's ideas as well as arguments for statehood. He feared that the country's identity was being lost under American influence, and like my mother, he embraced independence. I worried about that too. I was horrified when I learned as a teenager that half a million

Puerto Ricans had left the archipelago in a year. What did that mean for us as a country? We seemed to be losing a big part of ourselves, and it worried me deeply.

My father had several jobs as I was growing up. But the one he had for most of my adult life was at the Cooperativa, the town's credit union, which his father, Abuelo Ignacio, had helped found and where he was the manager for a long time. Earlier, he had inherited a jewelry store from my great-aunt Mamá Suncha and eventually opened his own pizzeria. In a small town like Vega Alta, the credit union was the local bank, so he knew everyone through his work there. People adored my father because he would go above and beyond the call of duty to lend them money. My mother would say that sometimes he even ignored bank policy to help people qualify for loans. My own ties to the credit union were deeper than I realized for many years. I was the third or fourth member because Mamá Suncha signed me up when I was born and put $3 a month into the account without my knowledge. It was only when I needed to buy a car as a student at the University of Puerto Rico that she told me about the money. "Just go and get a loan," she told me. So my first car was the result of what she had put aside, little by little, throughout my life.

In truth, she was not just a great-aunt. It was Mamá Suncha, as we called her, who had raised my father—not his own mother. It's not unusual in small towns for other family members to raise kids who may not be their own. I thought for a long time that she was my grandmother. It was only later that I learned that she had raised my dad because she'd never had kids of her own. She had also raised the children of her sisters as her own, looking after several of the cousins together. She married late in life, to a dentist from another town who already had his own child. She raised his child as her own as well. She was a businesswoman, running her own jewelry store and looking after her properties. Above all, she was very Catholic. I would go to church every Sunday because of her. If you did not go to church, she would know somehow, and she would call you during the week about missing church.

My actual grandmother passed away from cancer when I was four years old. It was a traumatic end. She lived in our town, and I remember her crying and screaming with pain—until it ended abruptly with morphine. People visited the house to pay their last respects, and their grief was real.

The home I grew up in was very simple, but in my mind, it was majestic. The house was in the middle of town, with a great porch facing the town plaza and Catholic church. We lived in the heart of the action. It was a single-floor wooden building, set on stilts, where the windows were just two shutters that we never closed. There was a big living room, four bedrooms on the side, a dining room, and a simple kitchen with a big counter facing the dining area.

Food was central to those early days in my town, and my favorite was an "empanada" or breaded meat. When I had my tonsils removed, an "empanada" was the first thing I asked for after the surgery—not ice cream, which would have been easier to swallow. We loved lasagna, made with Puerto Rican sofrito sauce—chopped cilantro, onions, cubanelle peppers, and garlic. When I tasted real Italian lasagna for the first time, I thought it was missing a key ingredient because the tomato base was so plain.

I grew up with my parents and my sister, Aurea Yamilla, who is almost five years younger than I. She was named after my grandmother, who died shortly before she was born. So nobody called her Aurea, and she goes by Yamilla. She looks more like my mother than I do, but we share something important: a sense of humor that we use to communicate the hard things in life. Our youngest brother, Elvin, came much later, when I was twelve years old. We lived together for only three years before I went to college, so we did not spend a lot of time together. I was the oldest grandchild on both sides of my family and was by some margin the oldest child in our home.

In my house, the first thing you would see when you walked in was a huge picture of Jesus Christ protecting the family. Mamá Suncha gave everyone a giant portrait of Christ when they got married, which no one liked. But out of great respect for her, and perhaps a little fear, nobody moved the giant Jesus. Ours portrayed him as the whitest man you could imagine, with his stigmata, praying for our souls. I remember pointing out to my parents that Jesus could not have been blond and blue-eyed, but it made no difference. My parents felt we needed to keep the picture in its prominent position even after they became Protestants. When we later moved to a cement home on the last street in town, the picture came with us, even though my mother repeatedly questioned why. My father's response was simple: "Because Mamá Suncha gave it to us." I never knew whether the picture eventually disappeared because Mamá Suncha passed away or because my parents changed religion.

———

I DID NOT WANT TO GO TO SCHOOL FOR FIRST GRADE. AS A THREE-year-old, I attended a one-class, private kindergarten run by a beloved teacher in my town. I loved it. My uncle Rodolfo, who went to school in the afternoons, spent the year helping in the classroom. But Mamá Justa and her family, including my uncle, were moving to San Juan.

Now I needed to face first grade alone. I wanted to stay at home like every other four-year-old in Vega Alta. My mother wanted me to go, but I cried and cried and cried and cried. My father explained to my mother that I could just stay in the house to read, watch TV, or play. My mother acquiesced, but she never forgot. For the rest of my life, she told me that I had wasted a year because they had not sent me to school.

When the time came to go to school at age five, I was both anxious and excited. School quickly became the center of my life. We did not have a lot of books at home, so when I wasn't with friends, I was at my local library. Our elementary school was overcrowded, so our schedules were staggered between a morning and afternoon shift. I always liked the morning shift so I could go to the library in the afternoon and just roam around, exploring whatever new books they had received. My parents noticed how often I went there, how much I loved books, and that I was fascinated by facts. The library was where I could fantasize about what was happening in the world beyond my small town, where everyone was in bed by nine in the evening and the TV screen turned to static snow two hours later.

One day when I was eight or nine years old, someone came to our house selling an encyclopedia called *El Tesoro de la Juventud*. It was not cheap, but I pleaded with my parents to get me the books. They indulged me, or were browbeaten by me, and paid up. Each week, I would wait anxiously for a new volume to arrive, when I would devour it. That meant I learned about the world alphabetically, reading each book from cover to cover. I learned about everything related to the As, and then the Bs, until I reached the final volume and the end of the alphabet. The most fascinating part was learning about so many countries, with their

different cultures and flags. I memorized each flag and could identify any country from its flag—as long as it had existed before
1966. When some African nations later gained their independence, I was lost. Still, that encyclopedia was my first big teacher,
opening the book of my imagination.

Above all, I wanted to excel, to do much more than I was asked.
In seventh grade, I needed to hand in a project in social studies. I
chose to document the Roman influence on architecture in Puerto
Rico. My poor dad traveled with me to more than twenty towns
where I would film the different types of columns with a Super 8
camera, declaring whether they were Doric, Ionic, or Corinthian.
What was wrong with me? I read *The Iliad* and knew all the classics. My teacher at the time said my expectations of myself were
warped. It was all so unnecessary, and yet, to me, it was all so
essential.

I loved school. I loved the challenge. I was the kind of student who loved all my teachers until my physics teacher entered
my life. I thought I knew more than he did. I felt that he was
making me waste my time and that I was learning nothing. My
father got very upset with me when I led an insurrection of the
students to get the school to change the teacher. He was a family
friend, just a guy from the town. Looking back, I can see how
my mother's high expectations created this impatience with anyone who knew less.

When I reached seventh grade, I was placed in a special group
of around twenty students who worked on an accelerated curriculum. Everyone in the group was really into school, and every single one of us went to college. The other kids called us names and
made fun of us as the chosen ones. But I have never given a shit
about what other people think of me. Other kids had friends who

played baseball. My friends were the kids who liked to do homework and play Ping-Pong.

My one release was the movies, and the small movie house in Vega Alta showed a different picture every day. We were always three or four years behind the general release, but that did not matter to us. I watched as many movies as my parents would let me see. My dad loved his Westerns, but they all looked the same to me. He also liked to read the pulp fiction known as novelas de vaqueros, which were the literary equivalent. They all had the same plot: there was always a good guy, like a sheriff, who kept the town in check by killing more people than anyone else, including all the Indians. I preferred the classics, but my tastes were eclectic. I must have seen *Ben Hur* twenty times, and I loved *Cleopatra*. I savored all the teen movies with Frankie Avalon and Annette Funicello.

It was at the movies, at an early age, that I fell in love with Debbie Reynolds and her bravura performance as the title character in the movie *The Unsinkable Molly Brown*. Watching that movie as a child was transformative. At one point, she's on the ground with her face in the dirt and a boot pressing down on her head, and she says, "Sure, I may be tuckered, and I may give out, but I won't give *in!*" Exactly, I thought. Molly Brown had dreams of something better, and so did I.

I knew I was very different when I saw *West Side Story* in Vega Alta's movie theater. At the end of the movie, when Tony is killed and Maria starts crying, my heart was in pieces. I was so upset. But as Maria started singing, the audience began booing and screaming that the movie was a piece of shit, and many left the theater. The concept of singing when someone had died was foreign to my neighbors in my town. I was just ten years old, but

I remember thinking that day, "Why am I different? Why am I moved to tears while my neighbors are pissed at the mix of tragedy and music?"

———

I GRADUATED FROM HIGH SCHOOL WITH A PERFECT GPA AT THE age of sixteen, a year early. Initially, I planned to study architecture. It seemed to have everything. I loved the arts, and I was good at math. I always thought that building things served a social function, which could be combined with an aesthetic sense of life. I would use both my quantitative abilities and my artistic sensibilities. Besides, I had loved building stuff as a kid with the Styrofoam that my father brought back from the Remington factory where he worked for a while. The challenge was that the University of Puerto Rico was, during those times of social upheaval, very political, and the schools of medical science and architecture were seen as places where students and teachers supported the status quo.

There was so much political change happening, but it was taking place in the social sciences and humanities. More than architecture, I wanted to be part of the movement. I could not decide between political science and psychology, but I felt haunted by the experience of my uncle Ernesto, the actor. Political science felt too unsure for my liking, whereas I could see psychology as a profession. I could make a living and have a real job. I was also influenced by the fact that my aunt Abigail was the dean of the psychology department. I already knew that they wanted to create a PhD program and figured that was where my life was headed.

My angle on psychology reflected my life's interests. During my second year of college, I leaned toward community psychology, working as an aide to a professor who was doing her dissertation in the field. We were assigned to a community that we were thrown into, and I picked the challenge of how to organize a community through theater. The community was in Cupey, where I knew no one. That year, I traveled there at least three afternoons a week and whenever I was free on the weekends. We set about creating a theater group with kids from the community and wrote a play about the issues facing them. The big challenge they faced was the lack of clean water, and we began organizing them to protest about it. That was when the program was shut down. It was one thing to create a theater group and stage a play with kids. But when it turned into a way for a community to fight for what it needed, we became a threat.

At least this type of psychology could help address systemic changes. I was always concerned about helping more people than you could possibly talk to one-on-one. I loved the idea of trying to solve problems for people when they got stuck in life, dealing with demons because of the shit that happened to them. I wanted to help them figure out how to get to the other side. My struggle with psychology was about how many people I could help in that way. Community psychology offered a way to solve problems at scale.

I already knew San Juan from my weekends with my grandmother and uncles. But college gave me my own community of people my own age, not the older generation. It was a much more varied community too, ranging from political activists to the pretty square kids from affluent families who did not send their children to study in the mainland United States. I may have come from a small town, but I was a fairly cosmopolitan kid who could help them with their homework and take them to my uncle's bar in old San Juan. All the students from Vega Alta arranged to meet for lunch regularly, but I went less and less to those meetings as I embraced a much wider variety of people, of different ages, from different places, studying different disciplines.

On top of my student life, I had a part-time job at Sears because I needed the money. I began in the summer of my high school senior year, one weekend, when they needed help with a project. It involved what I later learned were called intercepts, where you stop someone in the store and ask them a series of questions. I enjoyed it and asked for a part-time job, and they agreed to a position in the credit department. There were no computers in those days, so we were the place all the Sears stores called to check whether a customer could get the credit to buy merchandise—from clothes to a refrigerator. We would get on the phone with the customer, take down all their credit information, and make an initial determination, based on that conversation, of whether they were a good credit risk. Once you had their credit history, you could get on the phone and ask them why they were late with a payment and what was happening in their life at that time. People would tell you their story, and you would either believe them or not. It was a great deal of responsibility for a seventeen-year-old, but I thought I was much older because I was always hanging out with people who were much older. The credit department was full of freshmen, but they were probably two years older than I. Working late didn't bother me because I had spent all those late nights in my uncle's bar. The Sears doors closed at 9:00, but people were still buying stuff until 10:30 p.m., and you could not just throw them out. Soon, because I was always happy to be helpful, the supervisors put me in charge of scheduling everybody else in the department. I was eighteen years old, and I was managing the schedules of some two hundred part-timers and assessing the credit risk of thousands of Puerto Ricans.

A year later, they transferred me out to the store because I married my girlfriend. I had helped get a job for her in the department, and married couples were not allowed to work together. The credit department inside the store was the end of the road for the customer. It was the place you ended up when the kid on the phone could not make a decision about whether you were a good enough credit risk to take the refrigerator with you. Everyone who came to see me was pissed. They had probably spent hours on the shop floor trying to buy something, and now they had to explain why they were three months late one time, even though they had paid everything else on time. I was never fazed by the experience and encounters, no matter how angry they were. I always took the perspective that the big store was fucking with them. So many of those cases seemed unfair to me: the people were often good customers who had suddenly become unemployed because the factory in their town had closed. They were screwed, and it was not their fault. I was very sympathetic with the people I had to deal with. I knew what they represented, and I was worried about the erosion of Puerto Rico's economy because manufacturing was disappearing. I kept my cool, and so did most of the customers.

My attitude was noticed by the guy in charge of Sears in the Caribbean, and they started opening credit departments in other stores across Puerto Rico. Soon they asked me to fly to other stores to train the other part-timers. When I told them I wanted to go to New York to study, my bosses at Sears tried to convince me to study in Chicago, where they were opening a credit university. Their plan was for me to study in Chicago while still working at Sears before returning to Puerto Rico to resume a career with them. But I did not want to live in Chicago. I wanted to live in New York.

I HAD MET MY SWEETHEART IN SEVENTH GRADE, AND SHE HAD been my girlfriend since November 30 of that year. Brunilda Ocasio was a Puerto Rican transplant from Chicago. She had been born in the windy city, but her family was from Ciales, Puerto Rico. Upon their return, they moved to Vega Alta. We all thought she was unique because she spoke English and sometimes answered questions in English or in a kind of Spanish that we found funny. Her parents' relationship broke down as we finished high school, and her mother said she wanted to move back to Chicago when we were in our senior year. Brunilda did not want to return, and we convinced her parents to leave her behind with her godparents. That meant she moved to Bayamón, the neighboring town, and I did not drive at the age of fifteen. It was complicated, but I figured out how to travel to see her.

Brunilda was petite and beautiful, with a dark complexion. She worked hard, not just at Sears but also as an exercise instructor. She was very sweet, and we were extremely compatible. We had grown up together and were like brother and sister.

When we got to college, she lived in a dorm and I was living with my grandmother. It was not the best start for us. She was studying education and always wanted to be a special ed teacher. The next year, she got her own apartment with a friend, and we started having sex. At that point, I felt too much guilt. I was a good Catholic boy, and the church had done a great job of messing with my head. "We have to get married," I said to myself, "so we can continue to do this." And that was what we did, a year later. I moved into the apartment she shared with her friend, and then we got a place of our own.

My mother was outraged because she thought I was too young. She wanted me to finish school and work for a while. But my father was much more accepting. "You have your own apartment. You make your own money," he said. "You're probably sleeping with this young woman anyway. So go ahead and get married." For their part, Brunilda's parents were delighted at the idea of us getting married because their daughter was all alone in Puerto Rico. Now she would have someone to share her life with.

I convinced my mom it was fine, that it was what I wanted to do. So we went ahead with two wedding ceremonies. The first was to allow us to apply for an affordable apartment, so we had a quiet wedding just for the paperwork. Our big wedding was in August in San Juan. Even though I wanted to get married so we could continue having sex, my choice of priest was not simple. I was very involved in the pro-independence movement. The idea of a typical wedding was impossible. I wanted a Jesuit monsignor who advocated for the church to be an agent of change and for church doctrine to help oppressed people to rebel against their oppressors. For his revolutionary zeal, this monsignor had been thrown out of the church. So we had to find a place that would allow him to officiate.

Brunilda's wedding dress, made by a friend of ours, was very pretty and simple. It was a two-piece outfit, open at the back. She covered herself while in church, but once it was over, the dress was a simple little outfit. We had a great wedding, with a couple of hundred guests, including all our friends from Sears. It was not easy getting coverage that day for everyone at Sears because even our two supervisors came to the wedding. We honeymooned in Dorado, barely ten minutes away from my hometown.

A year later, I was on my way to New York.

IT WAS NOT JUST MY DECISION TO MARRY YOUNG THAT MARKED me as different in college. I embraced a radical form of politics. I certainly was not interested in statehood. To me, it never seemed to be a realistic idea. I had read enough and followed enough US politics to know that for the United States to acquire three and a half million "spics," with seven members of Congress and two senators, was never going to happen. People always point to the example of Alaska or Hawaii. But Puerto Rico is not Alaska or Hawaii. It's not dispersed communities of local people. It's a country, with its own language. In spite of hundreds of years of colonialism, the hearts of Puerto Ricans are stirred when they see the flag. I never thought the United States would give us representation, and I never thought we would want it. There was, and still is, a very active anti-American movement in Puerto Rico and a real affirmation of Puerto Rican identity in schools and across the country.

When I was a student, the Vietnam War was taking many of our kids, who left as soldiers and came back in coffins. We opposed the mandatory enlistment. I lived through two strikes at the University of Puerto Rico, including one that threatened my own graduation because the college was closed for so long. We demanded workers' rights, an end to the draft, and an end to increases in tuition fees. We were against the status quo, as all young people should be. The strikes always ended in violence. The one in 1970 left one student dead on the streets of Río Piedras and closed the university. For my part, I was not a revolutionary. I never drank the Kool-Aid, and I still don't, to this day. I never thought there was a movement strong enough to gain independence. It was strong enough to achieve other tangible things: to democratize the university, to allow more people to be educated.

But the ultimate goal of independence? In my head, it was not achievable.

I believed, then as now, that the main architect of statehood was in fact the PPD, which claimed to advocate for commonwealth status. It was actually supporting an entire economic system that reinforced our inability to exist without the United States. All it was doing was pushing statehood, even though that was not its stated intention. Every time someone gives a speech that we are American citizens, that we are entitled to this and that, they are pushing statehood.

We were struggling to figure out the next economic haven for the islands. If it was not manufacturing, it was the fuel-related industry, where oil was brought to Puerto Rico so we could do the dirty part of conversion and sell it to the mainland while polluting ourselves. Or it was tourism, where you depend on being nice to a whole bunch of people so they will come back. I have always thought it was cheaper to go to the Dominican Republic or to Cuba for the beaches and the palm trees and the nice weather. The arts have never been part of how we sell Puerto Rico, even though it has a lot of brilliant art and artists. We have theaters and museums that struggle because a critical mass of tourists or locals don't visit them. I have nothing against tourism as an integral part of economic development. But if you want to build an economy, you need to include everything a country has to offer.

I realized in college that independence was just a political solution. But what we needed in Puerto Rico was an economic solution. I was not interested in a capitalist country. What the Puerto Rican Socialist Party offered me was both a political solution and an economic one for working people. I was done with the Independence Party at the precise moment that my father was just embracing it. He would tell me there was nothing wrong with our economic system, that our problems started with the fact that everything was dictated to us by the United States.

"So the moment when they don't want to give economic credits anymore, our manufacturing dies," he would tell me. "If we were a republic, we could continue to give economic benefits to these companies."

"But Dad," I said, "I want the workers to be in charge. I don't want you to be in charge of the poor people in your own country."

In reality, I had been on this journey for some time. Several of my teachers in high school had been members of the Socialist Party. I had read about this economic system where the workers could be in charge. Once I was at the university, I began to read more and to go to meetings. Initially, I was part of the student Independence Party, but I soon joined the more radical group that evolved into the Socialist Party.

Yes, I worked for a big US corporation in the Sears credit department and also joined the Socialist Party. I was living the contradictions of capitalism and colonialism on the archipelago of Puerto Rico. But I never really worried about such contradictions. I always tried to figure out how I could fix them in another way. You sort of get that from the Catholic church: you sin, but you then go and pray several Ave Marias, and then you go sin again.

During my last year of college, I was finally old enough to vote. My own dad was running for mayor in Vega Alta as a candidate of the Puerto Rican Independence Party. But I campaigned for another candidate running for mayor for the Socialist Party. The candidate had been my theater teacher and had coached me when I competed to win the national award for the best monologue. My father was cool about the fact that I was working to defeat him. It was never an issue between us, and he never raised it. My mother complained to my sister but never confronted me either. My father was a saint.

"That's who you are," he said. "This is who I am."

Everyone in my family knew that the future for me was very clear. I was going to do my own thing, in my own way, in a place where you can cry with *West Side Story* but also be mad at it. A place where Molly Brown could go from poverty to abundance. A place where I could become the next best version of me.

CHAPTER 3

New Roots

I WANTED TO LEAVE PUERTO RICO. NOT FOREVER. I NEVER thought I was going to stay in New York—not for a nanosecond. But part of me wanted a bigger place to test myself. I couldn't complete a PhD in psychology in Puerto Rico. If I wanted to study law, there was a fantastic law school in San Juan. But psychology was different. All we had was a master's program, and there was already a fight for resources around that.

I was intrigued by the diversity of New York. The NYU psychology chair who recruited me, Bernie Kalinkowitz, had talked about his vision for a diverse school, where people brought very different experiences that would enrich the educational process. Back in Puerto Rico, my life was monolithic in terms of the kind of people who lived there. Our access to power and economic opportunities was limited by our country's colonial status. I had read so much about the melting pot, and now people were beginning to rebel against that idea. There was a pursuit of cultural diversity, and it was fascinating for me to go to a place that was ready to challenge itself. There was nothing better than New York. It was the ultimate challenge: like swimming in the ocean instead of being in your Puerto Rican lagoon. In my head, John Kander and Fred Ebb were right: if you could make it there, you really could make it anywhere. Then I could come back to Puerto Rico and make it there all over again. I was an eighteen-year-old who wanted to prove himself, even though I was a pretty mature teenager.

It was not my first visit to New York. I was ten or eleven when I first traveled there with my grandmother and my uncle. I saw the Coca-Cola sign in lights on Forty-Second Street and was mesmerized by the way the Coke disappeared as if someone were drinking it through the straw. Whoever dreamed that up? It looked like genius to me. The whole scene was one of those experiences that change you forever.

We stayed for a week in the city, just around the corner from Columbia University, living in a room we rented from a friend of my aunt: an Airbnb before the company existed. The subway took us directly downtown, where we visited every tourist attraction. We went to the Statue of Liberty and Central Park. I could not believe there was a castle inside the park. We saw a Broadway show and went to the top of the Empire State Building. To this day, I get goose bumps when I look at the Empire State Building. I come from a small town. It was a big deal to be in New York. The city was magnetic. And that has stayed in my head forever.

We were on a budget, so we ate in coffee shops. I could not believe there were so many different kinds of restaurants. In

Puerto Rico, there was Puerto Rican food. I knew of one Chinese place and one Italian place. But here in New York, there was an entire place called Little Italy and another called Chinatown, where you could order from a menu that made no sense to me.

A few years earlier, someone had given me a book of postcards of New York. You used to be able to buy them in tourist places, and you could tear one out at a time to send them back to your friends and family. In Puerto Rico, I vividly remember poring over these postcards and falling in love with a city I had never seen. There's a scene in *The Unsinkable Molly Brown* when Molly talks at length about postcards of Denver. I knew just how she felt because that was what I thought about New York. Did those places really exist, or were they Hollywood sets created for the movies? To come to New York and realize that those scenes actually existed was mind-boggling to me.

In spite of my love for New York, when the offer landed for the PhD program at NYU, I was undecided. I already had an offer to go to law school at the University of Puerto Rico and kept telling myself I could still go there if I wanted to. I kept both options open until the last possible moment, planning for both choices simultaneously. My father talked to his sister, who lived in Chelsea, and she began to set up the bedroom for my arrival. At the same time, I kept the door open to law school until July of that year—a month before I needed to be in New York.

I always kept many possibilities in my head, and the people who loved me knew that there was no point in offering me their opinions. They were excited for me when I finally made up my mind to come to New York.

I loved the city that I had dreamed about for so long. But I still wrote every day to everyone back home. I had no money to call people, so I wrote to everyone instead. I talked to Brunilda once a week and wrote letters every day.

I knew I would stay in New York from my first night in the city. But emotionally I still was not ready to leave Puerto Rico behind.

———

I QUICKLY REALIZED, AS A PSYCHOLOGY PhD STUDENT, THAT some of my experiences were not unique. There was a body of literature about Puerto Rican Syndrome, or ataque de nervios, describing the sort of outbursts that we have as Latinos, where people feel like they are possessed by a demon. I did not know it had a name. Today, it's the kind of name that would get you canceled. But if you look at it as a response to others, to dislocation, it merits further analysis. There was all this shit we were discovering on our own as Latino students, but we had no professor to help us explore it. There was absolutely nothing beyond the psychoanalytical crap that everybody had been talking about forever. There was no one who was willing to use that psychoanalytical framework to help us expand the literature. We could never assess whether Puerto Rican Syndrome was a racist label or a real condition unique to us. Fighting and protesting, to get attention from power, was one response to that. It was something I knew how to do. After all, I had been protesting against my teachers since at least my seventh grade physics teacher, who had taught me nothing.

Minority students were caught between the conflicting politics of our chair, Bernie Kalinkowitz, and his supporters who embraced quotas, and those who liked the old ways. We soon realized that what Bernie had done was truly revolutionary. It seemed clear that Bernie had been there for so long that he did whatever the hell he wanted. But the reality for Brown and Black students was that it was a half-baked experiment because the academic program was not changing to reflect the new student population. Nobody cared about Latino themes—at least, none of the professors did. The students could not get dissertation sponsors, and the classes did not speak to our reality. Other than our admission, nothing had changed in terms of the curriculum, the materials, or the faculty. If you wanted to succeed, you had to accept the educational status quo, and I couldn't.

We were not alone as psychology students at NYU. The same struggle was taking place for students of color across the city, and I was fully engaged. The flashpoint was the City University of New York, where student strikes and occupations had led to a policy of open admissions to any high school graduate, tuition-free. The demographics changed the university rapidly: there were 75 percent more students, and the proportion of Black and Latino students had doubled. The backlash was in full swing when I arrived in New York. Older faculty complained about falling standards. Conservative politicians complained about the cost. Funding was insufficient, and the expansion was chaotic. Open admissions faced an existential threat, and Puerto Ricans were at the heart of the struggle for bilingual education, quotas, teaching materials, and funding. My struggle with the slow change of culture in my university program was part of a bigger fight to change education across the city and the country.

I was part of a very active Puerto Rican socialist movement in New York. Our group met on the Lower East Side every Saturday. We sold our own newspaper, *Claridad*, and we studied Marxism together in someone's apartment. Many times, we met in my apartment to talk about the role of the Puerto Rican Socialist Party. Our discussions were repetitive between those like me, who cared about what was happening in Puerto Rico, and those who cared less. These discussions taught me about the need for a Black/Latino coalition. After all, we shared communities and were in the same boat. The Black activists wanted to fight for their community here in New York. If we did not fight for our rights together, who would? When and how would Democrats or Republicans fix the realities that we were facing? Nobody challenged the status quo, which was the reason why we lived in the worst housing, why we had the worst schools, and why no investment took place in our neighborhoods. The purity of the struggles began to change in my head.

We could mobilize thousands of people. But I learned very quickly that we were a fraction of the left, which included indigenous rights that I knew absolutely nothing about. I knew something about the Black American struggle, and of course a good amount about Puerto Ricans in New York. But I did not know much about the Mexican American plight and their fight for bilingual education and civil rights. To my shame, all I knew about Native Americans was that they were killed by John Wayne and had no rights. I had learned from the movies my father loved that they lived on reservations because John Wayne invaded those reservations and killed them all the time. Truly, I had no idea. All of a sudden, I discovered that the struggle for democratic rights was much bigger than ending colonialism in my little archipelago in the middle of the Caribbean.

It took me some time to understand. Of the five Latinos recruited into our program, the two of us from Puerto Rico knew a lot less about the Black American experience than the three Latinos from New York. They had attended Black and Latino schools. They understood the struggle, even though the Black students knew very little of the Puerto Rican struggle. It took me a little while to find the commonalities, but it finally struck me two years later, at the bicentennial celebration of the founding of the republic, when I found myself in the middle of the biggest protest of my life. We had massed tens of thousands of protesters in Philadelphia to call for an end to colonialism, economic injustice, racism, and discrimination. The causes that we were advocating for—the changes to the republic that we wanted—represented progress for many people. Puerto Rico, as the only modern-day colony left in the United States, was central to our protest. After two hundred years, wasn't it time for colonialism to end?

Those two years changed me profoundly. I saw that there was a struggle for democratic rights that many Puerto Ricans were fighting right here in New York. Until then, in my head, Puerto Ricans were like me—they all wanted to go back to the Republic of Puerto Rico. For Puerto Ricans in New York, there were things more important than independence: bilingual education, decent affordable housing, good health care. But I had not made the connection with electoral politics as an avenue for change.

At the time, NYU allowed students to do internships at the nonprofit Puerto Rican Family Institute, whose services included mental health care. I had two Puerto Rican patients, and I did not believe they could be interpreted just with Freudian psychoanalysis. I argued that we could not see someone four times a week and just put them on a couch to talk bullshit about everything since they were born. My patients had a lot of here-and-now issues that we needed to deal with. Yet nothing in my classes at NYU was about the here and now. They all went back to "Mami and me issues". Most of our supervisors would not support us talking about the real-world issues that Puerto Ricans faced in New York. The professors argued that resolving housing issues was important to patients' quality of life, but the "therapeutic relationship" was not the place for that. I could not have disagreed more.

When it came time to vote, my changing positions became clear. I was still voting in Puerto Rican elections because I had not changed my permanent residency. But by the time of my second election, I did not vote for the Puerto Rican Socialist Party. I voted for the party of my parents and uncle, the Puerto Rican Independence Party. I already knew that we could not convince Puerto Ricans to change their political status and their economic status at the same time. It was a nonstarter. So my dad was probably right: we needed to change the political status, which was the root cause of so many of our problems as a country. We could hammer out the economic reality later on. I even thought the United States would negotiate an agreement for our independence, since there would never be a full revolution on the archipelago.

Instead, the economic struggle I cared about had already moved to the mainland. The reality that now consumed me was a million Puerto Ricans who had such a hard life here. I was immersed in the day-to-day of Puerto Ricans and Latinos in New York. I could see how fucked up the buildings were and how the subway sucked—except for the lines that went through the rich neighborhoods. I wanted independence for Puerto Rico. But what would happen in the meantime to the million people who had left Puerto Rico? After all, their migration to New York and other cities in the United States was central to the changing economic conditions in Puerto Rico. With fewer people to support, fewer resources were needed.

———

MY POLITICAL EVOLUTION TOOK PLACE ALONGSIDE MY CAREER. I could not study in New York without working other jobs: I had my expenses and still had an apartment to look after in Puerto Rico. Soon after I arrived in New York, my aunt told me about the classified and wanted ads in the newspapers. She explained that there were many factories on Fourteenth Street, and because I had acted as a supervisor at Sears, maybe I could be a supervisor in one of those factories. Now, I had options. On my third day in the big city, I trekked uptown to Fordham Road in the Bronx to show my letters of recommendation to the Sears credit department there. Then I went to Fourteenth Street, to one of those sweatshops. The white owner I met there could not believe that I was some kid who had arrived a few days earlier. He certainly could not believe that I was in New York to earn a PhD.

"Listen," he said, "I have heard from the women who work here that there is a place that helped their kids. They're in education, and they give scholarships. And they help troubled kids like you."

In his analysis, I was troubled either because I was lying about the PhD or because I wanted to work in a sweatshop when I was a PhD student.

I went back to my aunt and recounted the owner's advice. She figured out that he was probably talking about a group called Aspira. So I took out the phone book and started looking for Aspira. There were three numbers: one on Fourteenth Street, another in Brooklyn on Court Street, and one on Fifth Avenue. Once again, my movie knowledge of New York City prevailed. I figured I didn't want to go to Brooklyn, but Fifth Avenue felt like I was moving up in the world.

I called to check that the group really existed, and then I just showed up. I went to the reception desk, and the woman there asked a few questions about me before sending me to the building next door. On the fourth floor was a newly established research department. It was there that I met the woman who would become my adoptive mother in New York, Dr. Norma Stanton. Norma was an Argentinian who had just moved from Boston to head this new research department at Aspira. She hired me on the spot. Later she explained that I reminded her of herself: she had come to the United States with very little English and even less fear of going into any room and opening her mouth. She was still conjugating verbs incorrectly when I met her, but it didn't matter. We were highly opinionated soulmates.

"I can only pay you three dollars an hour because I have to hire you like an intern," she explained. "But the moment something opens up, I'll make you an employee."

I remember calling my wife in shock.

"The streets are really paved with gold in New York," I said. I had worked at Sears for more than three years, and I was making just $1.85 an hour by the time I left. Here I was, in a new city, walking into a new job where I could earn so much more. I was obviously not in New York; I was in heaven! Three dollars!

It was my second week in the city, and I had already found the perfect job. When I walked out of the building, I would look up and see the Empire State Building, just like the postcards. I could speak Spanish but also practice my English with my coworkers. People would speak both languages and respond to each other in both, switching back and forth between them.

Our first task was to fight for open admissions, and my job was to gather the ammunition to make the best argument. I could not believe it. I was making almost double the money I had earned at Sears while learning about the struggles of Puerto Ricans in New York. I was researching at the great New York Public Library on Forty-Second Street, where two magnificent stone lions welcomed me every time I walked up the steps. It was just seven blocks from the office. Otherwise, I would research at NYU's majestic library, where I was struck by the internal space in the middle. This is a developed country—look at all of this wasted space. As a child, I had loved going to the library. Now I was getting paid to go to the most incredible libraries I had ever seen. On top of all that, the struggle for open admissions was clearly a fight for the civil rights of Puerto Ricans and Latinos. There had been open admission for everyone—including the Irish and the Italians—to open the door of opportunity. But the moment it was our turn, they decided to insist on tests and measurements and requirements. I had both a mission and a salary.

Aspira was my introduction to the nonprofit world, where I would work for several years and make friends for a lifetime. It was a collection of fantastic people: some were passionate about Puerto Rican identity and politics, while others just wanted to move on and move up. Politically, it was transformative for me, showing that you did not have to be proindependence to fight for the rights of poor people. Until that point, at least in my head, they were the same struggle. Aspira had started two decades prior when a group of Puerto Rican leaders had committed to developing the next generation of Puerto Rican leaders. They believed that the best way to free people from poverty was through education, leadership skills, and cultural pride. Aspira was meant to represent our own aspirations for a better life. There were Aspira chapters in high schools and colleges, recruiting young people to go through what they called the Aspira process of leadership, Puerto Rican history, and culture. It was a mixture of getting you in touch with your roots and building leadership qualities to make sure you changed the circumstances of your community. We were called Aspirantes, and our goal was to become educated and give back through politics, teaching, government, and community organizing. Education, opportunity, community: I became part of a movement whose values I already believed in.

Aspira introduced me to the world of program development, grant writing, budgeting, and management—all skills that would open new avenues in my life. I remember spending hours trying to define and quantify the Aspira process. It was a way to obtain resources from government and private entities to develop leaders, transfer culture to a new generation, and ensure that our kids had educational opportunities.

My enjoyment of the job was some compensation for my second thoughts about my psychology studies. I found the individual analysis of behavior boring, silly, and very middle class. There were eternal sessions about trying to figure out how you wanted to fuck your mom and how to resolve that conflict so you could enjoy a healthy balance between your superego, your ego, and your id. It was all very Freudian and unbelievable to me. I was spending hours learning about how communities were surviving in this city while studying at an elite institution about things that I didn't know how to use in real life. On one hand, there were people trying to figure out how to change housing conditions; on the other, there were people worrying about their relationship with their mothers. The first complex psychological phrase I learned was "cognitive dissonance." That was what I was living. The only two things that attracted me to my studies were my love of statistics and numbers and my love of psychological testing. I have always been a control freak, and statistics was a great way of trying to measure behavior. I could try to make sense of people's behavior quantitatively rather than listening to their bullshit forever. It was not that it was wrong; it just felt irrelevant. I was taking classes that bored me to death.

Eventually I became an adjunct faculty member at CUNY in what they called the miniversities—CUNY campuses in different neighborhoods. At the same time, a group of Puerto Ricans led by Dr. Victor Alicea had developed Boricua College, and I became one of its first faculty members, teaching social psychology and statistics.

The miniversities and Boricua College brought me closer to real Latino neighbors. The students were older and were giving themselves a second chance after working hard in New York to raise children. I learned about the perils and challenges of immigration. I learned what it meant to Puerto Rican families to leave their campos, their countryside, for la babel de hierro, as they call New York City. I learned that many of those who had been around for a while were still not part of the Democratic Party structure. Every single one of them knew more about politics in their countries of origin than the politics of New York. Again, there was such cognitive dissonance between my political sessions with younger people in the independence movement and community residents trying to echar pa'lante, to get ahead in New York City.

My interest in psychology was fading as quickly as my first marriage. Brunilda had not waited for me in Puerto Rico, where she had stayed to become a special education teacher. Instead, she had moved to New York in January 1975, transferring from the University of Puerto Rico to Lehman College to finish her last semester of study. We moved to an apartment in the Bronx on a street called Mount Hope Place. We called it Moho, like moldy shit, which was how our marriage was turning out. Five months after arriving, she told me she felt that she really had not experienced anyone in her life but me. That was true, since we had been dating since seventh grade.

I understood that she wanted to have other relationships, so I said we should get divorced. A week later, I moved out. I called my friend Nydia Velázquez, who told me about an apartment next to hers—a studio across the street from Cooper Union in the East Village—and I jumped at the chance.

When Brunilda told her parents about our separation, they freaked out. They asked me to go to Chicago to see if we could reconcile, and I did. We agreed to have therapy together, and that lasted all of two sessions. I was in the second year of graduate school, working an outside job that I loved. My life was great, outside my marriage, and I didn't want to fix it. By now, I had been in therapy for a year and a half, and that was very helpful because I had someone who could help me through the situation. We didn't spend countless hours talking about my mother (although we probably should have), but we talked instead about what I wanted to do in the here and now. So I moved out, got divorced right away, and never looked back.

———

I FOUND NEW DIRECTION IN THOSE EARLY YEARS IN NEW YORK, and that included meeting the love of my life. It was not an auspicious first meeting, to be honest. I was late because I had been caught in a protest at the United Nations, so I arrived a little histrionic and rattled. The police had cordoned us off, and we had been trapped. It reminded me of my days of protesting at the University of Puerto Rico. But there I was, late for a group interview with a new applicant to the PhD program named Luz. I met her briefly, heard just a little of her story, and then the student committee met to recommend candidates.

Luz had attended Livingston College, which was part of Rutgers University. It was an experimental program where grades were pass or fail. So in a school where the white students came from Harvard or Yale or Princeton and had all these fine scores, she had none. No grade point average. The students felt that she was unsellable to the larger admissions committee.

I remember saying something that would get you canceled today: "Did anyone look at her? She's one of the most beautiful women I've seen in my life. I think she should be around. We need her."

I'm afraid I might say something like that even now. There is always a bit of shock therapy in my arguments. I want people to pay attention, to get out of their comfort zone. Sometimes I may even say something outrageous that they are thinking but don't want to say. After that, I can appeal to them cognitively and emotionally with cogent arguments.

I pressed on, making the case that many colleges were experimenting with change. For sure, it was important that Luz had worked with Puerto Rican migrants in New Jersey to address their mental health needs. Her résumé was genuinely interesting and would provide a fresh perspective on the monolithic approach to mental health in our NYU curriculum. Fortunately, the student committee and the school agreed. She was accepted. I would later learn firsthand that in addition to being beautiful, she was brilliant and insightful.

This was the kind of student participation—with full votes as to who their classmates should be—that was incredibly avant-garde. It was an unbelievable laboratory for the way education should be. And needless to say, I had my head up my ass and couldn't see it back then.

The next time I saw Luz was at a party for her freshmen class. I was a third-year student and still thought she was the most beautiful woman I had ever seen. I went on my merry way, thinking she was way out of my league. We later had one class together, which was an experiential session that did not bring out the best in me. It was a class that I hated because it was one of those touchy-feely sessions where people had to say how they felt. I thought it was a waste of my time. I was challenging people all the time and calling them on their bullshit. In retrospect, I was horrific, but I believed I was always right. During one class, close to Halloween when I had a party to prepare for, I invented a fight in class just to be able to walk out and get my costume early.

A week later, I saw Luz.

"What was that all about?" she asked.

"I had to leave early," I said. "I had to get a costume."

"But you made everybody feel bad."

She saw right through me and called me on my own bullshit.

In reality, I thought Luz was unavailable. I knew she had a young daughter, and I naively thought that if you had a daughter, you were married. Maybe if I hadn't arrived late for her interview, I would have known the truth. Besides, by that point, I was splitting up with a very pretty, very witty woman I had been living with, because I was heading back to Puerto Rico. I had finished my coursework, and even though I hadn't finished my dissertation, I had gotten a job back home teaching psychology. I had even found a house where I was going to move.

My life was about to change direction once again. I just didn't know it at the time. Anita Soto, the wife of my best friend and an NYU student, invited me to the birthday party for her young son Sebastian. I was not a fan of children's parties, but Anita was very persuasive. We had gone to school together in Puerto Rico, and she was incredibly perceptive. "It's a typical Puerto Rican party: people of all ages," she explained. "And you know who is coming? Luz. And I know you like her." Now, Luz also had a young daughter, so she had a reason to be there. But Anita remembered that I thought Luz was the most beautiful woman I had ever seen, even though I had said it only once, two years earlier.

So I went to the children's party and spent the entire time talking to Luz. I learned that she had decided to have her daughter even though she was not married, had never been married, and had no intention of getting married. She'd had cancer when she was nineteen and got pregnant when she was in remission because she really wanted to be a mother. I was hitting my head against an imaginary wall because I had let two years pass by without asking out this gorgeous, smart, strong woman—and now I was going back to Puerto Rico.

A couple of weeks later, I invited Luz to our first date: a march in Washington outside the Supreme Court to protest the Bakke ruling that universities could not use racial quotas for admissions. Maybe it was not conventionally romantic, but politics have always been part of my DNA. I was planning to take the bus down from the Lower East Side, but Luz had a car. So we drove down together and stayed at the home of one of her cousins in Baltimore. We slept in separate rooms, and nothing happened other than us sitting on the lawn in front of the Supreme Court and me putting my head on her lap. She scratched my head and said she loved doing that. I later discovered that was not true. In fact, it was a total lie. But I do love people scratching my head, and I have been known to pay my children to do that. Did I fall in love with someone under false pretenses? It didn't matter. I couldn't get her out of my head.

The following week, I invited her to a concert of protest music by the Puerto Rican band Haciendo Punto en Otro Son at Washington Irving High School near Fourteenth Street. The band's name means literally that they make a different kind of music, because that was what we all wanted to do. Afterward we went dancing at a Latin place called El Corso on Eighty-Sixth Street and Third Avenue, where I used to go all the time. We spent that night together.

The next week, Luz helped me send my furniture back to Puerto Rico for my move back home. Two weeks after that, I called my mother to tell her I was not going back and that she should give away all my stuff. I was getting married instead, just four weeks after our first date. And she would soon become a grandma.

How was I so sure? I just knew. It's the way I live my life. When I'm sure about something, I go ahead and do it. I deal with regrets later. But let's figure out how to make it work. And if it doesn't work, I can't continue to bang my head against the wall.

———

WE WERE IN LOVE, BUT THE START OF OUR LIFE TOGETHER WAS not at all simple. I had given up my apartment and sent my possessions back to Puerto Rico, so I moved in with Luz in Somerset, New Jersey, where she lived close to her family. I was commuting to Williamsburg through the dreaded Holland Tunnel every day, to a new Aspira program in Brooklyn where I was doing psychological testing.

I had already decided that I would adopt Luz's daughter, Lucecita, or Cita for short. She did not have much of a relationship with her biological father. He was married when he fathered Cita, and I imagined his marriage was falling apart at the time.

On my second or third day of staying at Luz's place, Cita seemed unsure how to talk to me. She just said "you" this and "you" that. So I said, "Cita, I have a name. My name is Luis, and you could call me Luis."

"But I want to call you Daddy," she said. "I've never had a daddy like you are a daddy to me."

"You can call me Daddy if you want to," I replied.

"I can't," she said. "Because Mimi said that I should not get close to you."

Mimi was Cita's grandmother, and she had been helping Luz raise her for four years at that point. I was an intruder in a very settled family dynamic. It was a very, very rocky beginning.

Adoption laws in New York require the parents to relinquish their parental rights, even if they have no relationship and the child does not share their last name. So I had to meet Cita's biological father to ask him to give up his rights. I told him he could be involved in Cita's life as much or as little as he wanted. It didn't bother me either way; I knew I was going to have such a solid relationship with her that I wouldn't be threatened by his role. But little by little, he just walked away.

That was not true of Cita's grandmother, who wanted to exercise total control over Luz and Cita. She had been taking care of her granddaughter so that her daughter, who was living on student loans and food stamps, could go to graduate school. She resented losing control over them. When I walked into her house, everyone would look the other way. I would be left alone in a room, and nobody would speak to me. She even went so far as to meet secretly with Cita's biological father to convince him to stop the adoption; he declined.

I could not tell my parents that I was having so much difficulty with Luz's family. My mother never forgot and never forgave. She would remind my father not to help people who had slighted him decades ago. I knew I wanted to spend the rest of my life with Luz. I didn't want my mother resenting my wife's family forevermore.

Soon after, I remember driving and reaching a breaking point. I got home and said to Luz, "I love you. I want to marry you. But I don't need this shit. We either move to New York and put some geographic distance between us and your family to see if our relationship can work. Or I move back to New York, and it was a wonderful thing spending this time with you. I'm not going to live this life."

She responded without hesitation, "We're moving to New York."

The next week, we were living in New York City.

Life did not get easier with Luz's family, who agreed to spend Thanksgiving at our apartment in New York that year. They still refused to talk to me. I finally said the quiet part out loud: "Either I'm part of what's happening here in my home, or you all get the fuck out of here and we'll have Thanksgiving with just the people who are willing to be civil." Most of them walked out. It's very difficult for me not to say what I think. But I also know that I'm not easy, and I'm sure it wasn't easy for them when I showed up and suddenly there was a wedding.

We were married three months after we started dating. Cita's biological dad showed up with someone he had just met. Luz's parents arrived at the last minute—not quite late and just in time for the ceremony. It would take another three years before Luz's mother apologized for thinking the worst of me. Luz told me that was the first and last time her mother said she was sorry to anyone for anything. So I should consider myself very fortunate. As Rubén Blades wrote in "Pedro Navaja," "La vida te da sorpresas." One of those surprises was that I would end up caring for Mimi in our home during the last eighteen months of her life. It's difficult for me to hold grudges. Life is too short.

AS REMARKABLE AS OUR WEDDING WAS, IT STILL DIDN'T FEEL RIGHT for Luz. She had gone to Catholic schools run by the nuns, having grown up in a privileged, middle-class home. Her father was a successful mechanical engineer and the first Mexican American to graduate from the Merchant Marine Academy at Kings Point. It was important for her to marry in church, but I was a divorced man and could not do that. Still, she was relentless and would dress as a bride every Halloween. Even when she was pregnant with Lin-Manuel, she dressed like Miss Piggy in a wedding dress.

I kept telling her that it was silly because it meant I would need to get an annulment. I had loved that part of my life with Brunilda. Even though it had ended badly, I didn't want to pretend that it hadn't existed. Still, it was important to Luz. I started the process years later when I was working for Mayor Ed Koch, who was good friends with Cardinal O'Connor, the archbishop of New York. Whenever they got together, they would bring in some Catholic staff, and I was always one of them. One day I asked the cardinal about the process for an annulment and told him my story. One of his staff called me to start the process. But it involved reaching out to Brunilda. I called her godparents, who still lived in Puerto Rico, and they gave me her number. We had not talked in years.

"I need to get an annulment," I began. "They're going to send you some papers. I'm sure you'll have no problem because you've been married since. I'm marrying the only other person I want to marry in my life."

She never agreed to the annulment. But I had made a good-faith effort, and with the passing of time, that was enough for the church.

Luz and I were finally married in the Lady Chapel in St. Patrick's Cathedral by Cardinal O'Connor himself. By this time, Cita was eighteen years old and Lin-Manuel was twelve. It was late March, and there had just been a huge snowstorm. In the madness of planning the wedding, alongside our busy working lives, I had forgotten to book a car to take us from the cathedral to the reception. So we walked from Fiftieth Street the dozen or so blocks to our reception: the entire wedding party, led by Luz in her wedding dress—the dress that had belonged to her mother—walking down the middle of Fifth Avenue to our party. As we took over the street, we passed one woman who stared at us in disbelief, saying, "Now I have seen it all."

CHAPTER 4

Getting Schooled

I LEFT PSYCHOLOGY AT THE AGE OF TWENTY-THREE WHEN I realized that I had no patience for how slowly the therapeutic process works. One day I was with someone I had been seeing each week for two full years, and I thought we were making progress. He worked for city government and talked about living a miserable existence. He had real issues with intimacy and found it hard to be close to his friends and to women. It was a struggle for him. I listened, week after week. At long last, he was dating a woman he liked and who liked him. During the sessions leading to their first intimate date, I was delighted at being able to see his progress. He told how they finally got in bed together and were about to have sex. This was the first intimate sex he'd had for a very long time. He had been with prostitutes, but this was different. He told me that, as he got into bed with her, he saw a hair on her chest. That triggered all sorts of homosexual fears—issues we had been dealing with for two years. So he failed to have an erection, and the encounter ended in misery.

When that session ended, I said to myself, "I cannot do this job for the rest of my life." Even during the session, I stood up and said, "Could you just go and pluck the hair and move on with your life?"

All of my teenage fears about dealing one-on-one, about failing to change the world, were crystallized by this one patient and this one strand of hair. I was still at NYU, completing my PhD program, and I knew my psychology career was over because, honestly, it was not what I wanted to do with my life.

Of course, I knew that much of the problem lay within me. I had been in therapy since the moment I had arrived in New York. I had always been reflective about my life and my issues. Back in Puerto Rico, I had talked to counselors whenever they were available. But once I came to New York and started my PhD, I was in therapy within a month. It was highly encouraged for anyone studying clinical psychology, and I found a fantastic guy who was just like my dad. I had been in therapy twice a week for four years when I realized that psychology was not my dream job. On top of that, all of us were in supervision, making sure that our own issues did not interfere with our relationship with the patients.

In reality, it should not have been a surprise. One professor had already said to me in one solo supervision, "You are not cut out for this." My reaction was not good. I told him he was racist, but in retrospect, he was the only person who told me the truth. All the other professors went along with the pretense because I was smart and I worked hard. But this one professor knew that I was not good for this kind of psychology. He said I always wanted to rush the therapeutic relationship, pushing my patients to do more than they could. Why not? That was the story of my life: move on, be the best, process fast.

"Why do you want me to listen to their bullshit week after week?" I asked. "My job should be as an agent for change."

"You don't do this to be an agent for change," he replied. "You do this to help people get better at their own pace. Not at yours."

"That's a waste of time," I said. "A fucking waste of time."

I thought people would appreciate accelerating the pace of change. He had the guts to tell me that the only person who would appreciate it was me—because I could be done with them and move on to the next patient.

He was right. But it would take me years to understand that.

I never finished my PhD, even though I went as far as writing three chapters of my dissertation, creating a committee, collecting my data, and putting them all on punch cards for one of the early computers to read. Only to end up saying to myself, "I don't want to do this."

My dissertation was about the very issues I was grappling with in real life: what kind of identity do you have when you are caught between two cultures? The official subject was the effects of acculturation on the self-concept of Puerto Ricans. We measured acculturation by Puerto Rican knowledge and tastes, giving people a score for that as well as the notion of self-concept. I borrowed the measure of Puerto Rican acculturation from another student at NYU who was several years ahead of me. The control group was in Puerto Rico.

What I found was that the more you were at either end of the acculturation spectrum—either a little or a lot—the higher your self-concept was. In other words, the less doubt you had about who you were, the better you felt about yourself. I gathered all the data, performed all the tests, wrote several chapters, and even took the comprehensive exam to graduate. I did all the tough stuff. But it just was not what I wanted to do with my life. Finishing felt fake and anticlimactic.

You have no idea how much Luz tried to convince me.

"Just be a doctor," she said. "Write one more chapter and defend your dissertation."

"Honey," I replied, "maybe someone will give me an honorary degree at some point in my life. If you want to call me doctor, you can call me doctor then. But this is a farce. This is not what I want to be a doctor of."

With that, I closed a chapter of my life.

———

LIN-MANUEL WAS UNPLANNED, MUCH LIKE THE REST OF OUR lives. But his arrival came at a tricky time because Luz had just been accepted for an internship at the Jewish Board of Children and Family Services, which serves diverse communities in need across the city and had an infant program. (Two years later, she reapplied and completed her internship.)

"It's totally up to you," I said. "We're going to be married for a long time. We could have more kids."

"No, no," she said. "I know I have that option."

It was just the second year of our married life together. Cita was about to turn six in November. But Luz decided to go ahead with the pregnancy even though it was high risk. She had suffered thyroid cancer eight years earlier, and the surgery had damaged her parathyroid glands. She had been on medication ever since, and I was changing jobs, so we were living without medical coverage.

That forced us to go through a midwife program at Roosevelt Hospital because it was affordable.

Lin-Manuel was born on January 16, 1980, without any complications for mother or baby. Luz was twenty-eight, and I was twenty-five.

Now with two children, I realized that I needed to figure out what I was going to do with my life, since for so long I had defined my life as wanting to be a psychologist. That was when I started doing an assorted number of jobs, beginning with New York's Department of Employment. One of the top people at Aspira had been appointed assistant commissioner for youth employment, and the city had secured a chunk of money from the Youth Employment Act. She asked me to join her there. "We want to conduct a whole bunch of research with all of these new dollars and new programs that we're getting," she said. I believed the only real skill I had developed from pursuing my PhD, and that I enjoyed, was research and statistics.

It felt like a comfortable transition out of psychology. Aspira was like a family to me. Now I was in a room with hundreds of desks in the big government building where the Department of Employment lived on Church Street. I couldn't hire anyone from outside because people needed to take civil service tests. So I was stuck with a lot of people I never would have hired if I'd had any real power. It was a big job, but I had to hire from within. They were also letting go of many people at the time, so I also knew that the people I didn't hire would most likely get fired. I was twenty-six years old. Making these big decisions that directly impacted people's livelihoods was new for me. I had nightmares constantly.

My team was average, and everyone was much older than I. But I quickly learned that everyone could do way better if you challenged them and treated them the right way. If you showed respect when you supervised them, if you expected jobs to get done and people to work hard, they were no longer civil servants who would say, "I cannot be fired." They really worked, and 5:00 p.m. was no longer the time when everyone went home—because there was still more work to finish. It was amazing.

Our job was to figure out the components of these new programs, especially around compliance. These were highly regulated programs, and the money needed to be accounted for. The city was emerging from a fiscal crisis, so there was a lot of focus on what was happening to the money, what the contractors were doing, and what the outcomes were. These were all skills I had learned at Aspira. This was not social research as I had learned it at NYU, with control and experimental groups. We needed to make sure that the programmatic goals were achieved and help set up protocols to provide data on goals. This was the technical work of a bureaucracy. It was also the work of an adult. With two children, living in a one-bedroom apartment, we needed to move on.

New York City was our home now. I was working in city government and began to attend meetings of the Democratic Party just to hear what was going on. I started following the mayoral race for the first time in my life. And I was teaching four nights a week at CUNY's miniversity and Boricua College. I still followed Puerto Rican politics and even sold *Claridad* from time to time. But the Puerto Rican Socialist Party did not make much sense anymore. My job was not even Latino-centric but instead involved ensuring that disadvantaged people could acquire the skills they needed to enter the labor market.

Soon I was offered a new job that meant much more to me but also strained our family even more. My new mission was running the research work for the National Action Council for Minorities in Engineering. It was a very well-funded nonprofit supported by companies that wanted to hire more minority engineers. There was an abysmal number of people of color who were engineers, and that included more Latinos than African Americans—because the large companies would go to Puerto Rico to recruit from the engineering school in Mayagüez. That is why, for instance, there is a large Puerto Rican community in Rochester: because Kodak used to hire twenty-five or thirty graduates from the Mayagüez engineering school each year.

The job involved much more sophisticated research than the one at the Department of Employment. It paid more, but it also required a lot of travel. It involved going to universities, setting up research protocols on math and science skills, collecting data across the country, meeting with deans, and measuring retention results. We were giving real resources to send minority students to these schools, and we wanted to know whether the programs were succeeding. One of the main difficulties holding back both Latino and Black high school kids was that if their schools offered anything, it was algebra. Without trigonometry or calculus, they did not have the foundation for engineering school. Some of the programs began in ninth grade so they could follow their math sequence to reach calculus in their senior year. It was an interesting job, and the organization was ambitious. It had just secured a huge grant and wanted to double the scale of what it was doing.

These were the days before GPS told you how to navigate around the world. The work helped me grow even deeper roots in the United States, traveling to places I never would have seen or understood otherwise. But it was also an enormous challenge to rent a car at the airport and try to figure out with a paper map where I was going. Most of these places did not have taxis, and back then, there was no Uber either. I packed a big atlas of the metropolitan areas of the United States and spent hours trying to figure out how I would get from the airport to my destinations.

When Lin-Manuel was born, I did not know how long we could sustain my travel. I could pack my trips into a couple of days, taking red-eye flights back from the West Coast. I would organize double the number of meetings a normal person would have so that I could get back to my house more quickly to spend time with my baby and my seven-year-old daughter. But we needed another solution, and her name was Edmunda Claudio, or Mundi, as everyone called her.

Mundi had been my nanny in Vega Alta, hired by my mother when my sister was born. One day, just before Lin-Manuel arrived in our lives, Mundi was visiting her daughter in Connecticut when she decided she didn't want to stay in Puerto Rico. We had arranged a job for her with a friend when Luz really started to struggle with her pregnancy. Lin-Manuel dropped in the last two weeks and hit her disc; Luz could not move and needed help to go anywhere. So Mundi moved in with us, and then, when Lin-Manuel showed up, she fell in love.

We told her we could only pay her $100 a week and give her room and board. But she insisted that she didn't need the money and didn't care about the money. She would be part of our family until the day she died on a Christmas Day.

She is the inspiration for the character of Abuela Claudia, who raises the young Usnavi and the rest of the barrio, in *In the Heights*. When she went to see the show, she told Lin-Manuel with her usual mix of wit and sarcasm, "You killed me! I won the lotto, and then you killed me."

It was an important part of the plot, but she did not appreciate it.

Mundi had old-school opinions. She had known me since I was four years old, and she frankly thought that Luz was not a good enough wife for me. Luz was a good woman and a great mom, to be sure. But not a 1950s housewife. Mundi's job, in her mind, was to do all the things that Luz should have done—like dressing Lin-Manuel to go to school or being at my beck and call. One day I got home and saw Mundi's face: she was glaring at Luz and ready to let loose.

"Are you going to give dinner to your husband?" she asked Luz.

"I don't serve dinner to my husband because he has two very able hands, and he can serve himself," said Luz. "But I take care of this." With that, she walked up to me and grabbed my crotch. Mundi laughed and said, "Fresca." She promptly stood up and served me food.

Mundi had come of age in an era when women were there to take care of men. It just wasn't Luz's philosophy. With time, Mundi learned to love Luz and told me many times (but never to Luz), "She's a keeper."

It was like having a grandmother in our house—except that there were now five of us in a one-bedroom apartment. Mundi shared a bunk bed with Cita, while Luz, Lin-Manuel, and I shared the living room–bedroom. There was not a clear line between a living room and a sleeping room. When Lin-Manuel began to walk, he would carry a little futon around with him and fall asleep wherever he wanted. If he wanted to sleep in the kitchen, he would put his mattress there and go to sleep. When my mother saw that for the first time, she jokingly threatened to call child services on us. But we were very lucky to have Mundi in our lives. Luz and I were young and working hard to build our careers. I was taking lots of consultancy jobs to try different things now that psychology was a thing of the past. Luz had to stop work on her degree to have Lin-Manuel. Everything was possible if we just worked a little harder.

While the employment job had put me in contact with local politics in New York City, the engineering work expanded my horizons nationwide. Little by little, I learned about blue, red, and purple states. Working with so many school districts, I could see firsthand the disinvestment in public education for Black and Brown kids everywhere.

———

Luz was desperate to buy a house for our family, as our lease at the university housing had expired. I would have been fine with a bigger apartment, but Luz had grown up in a house. Now we were under the gun to move to get some more space. In 1981, the real estate section of the *New York Times* listed houses for sale in New York City. After reading an article on affordable neighborhoods in the city, Luz spotted a listing for a house in Inwood, in northern Manhattan, for $75,000. It included a rent-controlled apartment on the second floor. Crime was high, though lower than in some parts of New Jersey, but I wasn't really interested in looking at the statistics. I just knew that the A and the 1 trains were right there, taking me anywhere in the city that I loved. I could stay in New York City rather than moving to New Jersey.

It wasn't easy raising the money for the $25,000 down payment: we borrowed from many family members. Interest rates were running sky-high at 19.25 percent. But we scraped the money together and bought the house, which needed repairs. We did not mind.

Coming from a one-bedroom apartment, it felt like heaven. We still live in that house to this day.

That's not to say the neighborhood was entirely happy to see us. Certainly not the lady who was about to become our tenant. Until that point, Luz had been the main point of contact, and she used the name Towns rather than Towns-Miranda. She has no accent, and people assumed I was Mr. Towns. Then I showed up at the Irish tenant's door, and she heard my accent.

"Where are you from?" she asked.

I explained that we had been living in university housing in the Village.

"No, no, no," she said. "Where are you from? You're not from the Village."

"I'm from Puerto Rico," I said proudly.

"You don't have to worry," she replied without missing a beat. "I'm not going to have spics as my landlord. We're moving out."

Perhaps she thought she was going to get kicked out anyway. But we had no intention of moving her out of her rent-controlled apartment. She didn't realize that she would be dealing with decent people. Nor did she want to believe in the idea of decent people from Puerto Rico. So we moved upstairs, which was a bigger apartment where everybody could have their own room, and Luz turned the downstairs into her private practice.

Our fortunes changed with a twist of bad luck. One day I was in a taxi, on the way to my doctor for an annual checkup, when my cab was hit by another car. It was a serious accident. I was banged up inside the taxi, and the driver was pinned between the steering wheel and his seat. I wasn't paying attention when the impact happened, so I just bounced around. The fall was awkward, and my leg was broken. We waited for the police to arrive, and the officer wanted to call an ambulance. But I was just a few painful steps away from my doctor's office. The doctor said I was very lucky and put me in a cast for three months. I would try to navigate the subway on crutches, but many times, Luz drove me to where I had to work.

One day I saw an ad for one of those 1-800 numbers for lawyers, and I called them up. They sued the cab company for me, since I was the only one involved in the accident who had absolutely no responsibility. We eventually won $75,000 in compensation, and the lawyer kept one-third. With the remainder, we could afford to pay back everyone who had lent us the money for the $25,000 down payment. As they say in my town, No hay mal que por bien no venga. The silver lining in that cloud was worth a lot.

For me, moving to the Heights was like moving back to Vega Alta. It was a community, even though there was a different mix of people.

You walked around our neighborhood, and every store had music blasting. You went to a restaurant, and there was music blasting. It was hard to find a restaurant in our neighborhood where you could speak. Music was woven into our lives. Cita took piano lessons and so did Lin-Manuel. Neither Luz nor I could play, but we both loved music, and our house was always full of tunes. We listened to show tunes and salsa; Mundi listened to boleros; Cita listened to hip-hop.

Our community also took shape around local politics. I knew one guy in the neighborhood through Aspira, so I told him I was moving there and wanted to start getting involved locally. He told me they were putting together a slate of parent candidates to defeat the candidates of the United Federation of Teachers on the local school board. Parents in our district were immigrants and could register only as parent voters. During those days, school boards hired and fired school leadership and had access to hundreds of non–civil service jobs—but our schools sucked. Cita was already going to Mott Hall, one of the local schools, and Luz and I were attending the parents' meetings. Our neighborhood, District 6, was the lowest in the city in math and reading scores. It was also overcrowded, with the schools running at 180 percent of their capacity.

After a year and a half of traveling all over the country, I changed jobs again to something that was much more settled. I was tired of spending so much time on the road, and I missed the kids. I was losing so much by being absent for such large chunks of time, and I wanted to be more involved—in our family and community. I started work at the Community Service Society, doing research and advocacy on youth employment. It blended my experience in the Department of Employment with my work on minorities in engineering. Now my only trips were to Albany, the state capital, because we needed to figure out legislation at the local level for everything we did. It was my first real immersion in partisan local politics.

So I was more than ready for the political fight for control of the school board. At my first meeting in one of the schools, there were maybe ten or twelve parents. I spoke like a politician, mobilizing the masses into action. After that, my wife and I started meeting with the presidents of all the parents' associations in the district, and we started organizing the parents. We met leaders like Guillermo Linares and his wife Evelyn. Our message was clear: until we organized and elected the right people, our kids would not be a priority. The UFT grew very anxious about what we were doing. The school board exercised real power at the time:

appointing principals and the superintendent, approving budgets, and creating the structures for the education system. The UFT wanted to make sure its own people were in positions of power.

We began to pack auditoriums and board meetings. Nothing else I've done in my life felt more powerful and effective than mobilizing hundreds of parents to take over their schools. The opposition just had to turn out the voters to go to the polls. We needed to register noncitizens who can vote in school elections, regardless of their immigration status. We were organizing people for something that was very real. And our message to the community was urgent: you came to this country because you wanted a better life for your kids. You cannot stay at home. It doesn't matter if you're undocumented. They're not going to arrest you at a board meeting.

We created councils of parents and parent presidents of all. the schools. The UFT hated us: Luz and I were really unwelcome as far as the union was concerned. Luz became the president of our parent association at Cita's school, and I was one of the rabble-rousers. Closets were being transformed into places where special ed kids got their one-on-one services. It was bad, and we documented it and took photos. Parents had private interviews with staff, and we obtained the recordings. We took all this evidence to the meetings. Even our social life revolved around the mission. We often met at the Asociación Comunal de Dominicanos Progresistas (Community Association of Progressive Dominicans) and spent every weekend at its activities. Cita and Lin-Manuel would hang out with neighborhood kids their own age.

The district superintendent was sympathetic to our plight. But she was trying to be fair and cautious, to hedge her bets. When I met with her, I told her, "They're going to fire you. The only way you keep your job is to help us. You know that when they win, they are firing you. So you could start packing, or you could start helping us. You know we'll help you do your job and provide the services our kids need and deserve."

"What do you want me to do?" she replied.

"Appoint a parent rep in every school. You already have these positions in the books. Let's have a person in every school. That person's job will be to help in the school cafeteria and all that shit. But they're also going to register parents. That's their job. And when the election comes, their job is to make sure they call parents. They don't need to tell them who to vote for, but they will tell them to come out and vote. You figure out how you combine the work and the activism. We have great parent candidates for you to hire for every school."

We called ourselves the Community First slate, and we became a force to be reckoned with. Our goal was simple: representation for parents to take over the education of their kids. There was not one Dominican principal in the district, even though Dominicans represented 80 percent of the student population. We created a network of school workers who organized the parents. That year, we registered more parents in District 6 than in the entire city of New York. We registered ten thousand parents to vote in that election, and we developed friendships with neighbors who would later run for office themselves.

School board elections were decided by ranked-choice voting. You voted with a number 1 next to a name, then a 2, and so on. That meant that, in addition to having our candidates, we added to our slates the names of other candidates who were also running—but not on our own slate. When the opposition candidates dropped out of an early round of the count, their votes came to our candidates. We relied on parent organizers who were passionate about what they were doing. One friend of mine, the parent president of PS 132, Felicia Peguero could jump on a table and organize two hundred people. Her husband Viterbo owned the local bodega, and we operated out of his store. We were part of the fabric of the neighborhood.

When the election was over, we ended up with a divided board, and we then had to negotiate a path through the complicated subcultures of New York politics. We elected four members of the school board, while the UFT elected four. The remaining seat was elected by the Jewish Community Council, which typically voted with the UFT. There had long been an Orthodox Jewish community in Washington Heights, with a synagogue on 187th Street. Their children did not attend the public schools—they went to their own yeshiva schools. Still, the UFT looked after them by appointing Jewish members of the community to positions of power.

Our objective was always clear: create better schools, relieve overcrowding, appoint educators to positions of power, and embrace diversity. To do all that, we knew we needed to get the Jewish Community Council on board. I was trying to be a consensus builder, so I met with the council a thousand times. In particular, I worked hard to win over my local councilman, Stan Michels, who saw us moving into the neighborhood and packing the school meetings, which had never happened before. I learned to love Stan. He came to one of our meetings and said, "I want to meet with you."

"I want to meet with you too," I said.

We became great friends, and Stan convinced the Jewish Community Council member to support us at the school board. He quickly resigned. Now we had one open seat, which meant four versus four on the school board. It was progress, but it was also a nightmare. Power was divided, and we had total gridlock. Our board members protected our friendly superintendent, but the UFT began to make life miserable for her.

Systemic change is possible when you fight to get inside and work within the system to change it and make it fairer. School board elections felt like a fight, but in the end, we elected half of the board members, and we worked with an established superintendent and started making the changes we thought were needed for immigrant kids to be seen and served.

Compromise was no longer possible. We changed our strategy and sued the school board with the help of our lawyer Michael Rebell. My daughter and I were the plaintiffs, and we went to see the Board of Education's chancellor. We told him we wanted to remove the board. All four of the members we had elected were in favor, and the chancellor removed the whole board. In their place, he appointed three trustees to clean up the schools.

That was how I came to the attention of City Hall. Because I was trouble.

In the end, the kids won: we got nine schools built in the district. I emerged with great relationships, even with my opponents, like Sandra Feldman, the head of the UFT. I told her we could work together—and we did for years.

If the Orthodox Jewish community complained, we listened. When the time came for us to build a school near their yeshiva, they objected that it was opposite their school. I guess they feared the Dominican kids might interact with their kids. It made no sense. But people have fears, and even unfounded fears feel real. What were we supposed to do? Psychoanalyze them to make their fears go away? No, the answer was to negotiate what was acceptable. We could not engage in an ongoing fight with people who had as much right to live in the neighborhood as we did. We could not fight for our rights while denying the rights of others. In the end, the solution was very simple. We just made the entrance doors of the school on the side of the building, rather than the front. So the kids were going in and out of different streets, and the backyard, where the kids played, was what really faced the yeshiva. For some, this was selling out. But the school was built, and the Jewish leadership was happy.

————

WE NAVIGATED DIFFERENT CULTURES ACROSS THE CITY, NOT JUST in our activism but also with our own children. When Luz and I were at NYU, Cita went to a Montessori school in Greenwich Village with friends from the neighborhood whose parents owned their own town-houses. I learned about the concept of playdates, which I had known nothing about. Back in Vega Alta, you just showed up at someone's house. Cita's social circle changed dramatically when she moved schools to Mott Hall in Washington Heights and later Stuyvesant High School at its old location on Fifteenth Street. Lin-Manuel lived a very different life at Hunter College Campus Schools on the Upper East Side. The logistics of school choices were always complicated.

At Stuyvesant, Cita mixed with kids who came from all over the city. It was academically excellent, but admissions were based on testing, so the students were drawn from many different neigh-borhoods. Only a few were accepted from uptown, and she felt a bit isolated. Cita's friends were the handful of Black and Latino kids in the school, and she found the place much less friendly than her life in the Village.

The world of parenting is tricky, particularly when it comes to raising adolescents. Luz had grown up in suburban New Jersey, and she was a very protective mother. Her favorite word is "no." Cita learned as a teenager to ask me if she could go somewhere. I was the parent who would say yes. But then there was a high school trip that I approved despite her mother's objections. There were chaperones and teachers, so I thought it would be fine. Of course, it became an incident: it turned out that a group of kids were drinking and vomiting on the bus. I lost the moral high ground forever after that. I still get shit about that incident from Luz.

It was very different for Lin-Manuel at Hunter, where he was very happy with the same friends for years. The kids were so smart. (They were tested for admission for forty spots.) The most amazing part was hearing those kids speak among themselves: they were so verbal, negotiating everything as if they were little adults. They would talk about culture, politics, and their feelings. I was always perplexed that these little children could talk like that.

Lin-Manuel was such a good kid that parents would call to ask for playdates with him. We didn't know whether the children also wanted him to come over, but parents loved him. They picked him up from school to take him to the East Side or the West Side. Nobody wanted to come uptown. We would just show up at 6:00 p.m. to collect him on our way home from work. On a sleepover, Lin-Manuel fell on a skateboard and lost his front tooth. The mother of his friend called to tell us what had happened and that she was already on her way to the dentist. It was a Saturday, and the dentist was opening up especially for them. Lin-Manuel came home with $5 from the Upper East Side tooth fairy, which was considerably more than the quarter he would later get from the tooth fairy uptown. The first time we ever went to the Hamptons was with the family of another of Lin-Manuel's friends, who lived on the West Side.

To this day, Lin-Manuel likes to tell the Christmas story of going to Macy's to take a photo with white Santa Claus and then coming uptown to have a Brown Santa celebrating with the kids on the corner of 175th Street and Amsterdam. Hunter was a very different community, but we loved the people there, and they were very supportive. When Lin-Manuel started his career with the first *Freestyle Love Supreme* show at Ars Nova back in 2001—before all of the hype and before *In the Heights*—there were six or seven mothers of his Hunter school friends who showed up to his first performance. I was so moved that I hid in the bathroom to shed a tear. He is still friends with all those kids who shared his class from kindergarten to high school.

Lin-Manuel was a very different kind of child. He was a smart kid and was reading by the age of three. Mundi and I would speak Spanish with him, while Luz and Cita would speak English. By the age of four, he could read in both Spanish and English. That was no small part of the reason he hated Cita's Montessori school in Greenwich Village: the other kids were jealous of his reading. He was struggling, so Luz found a local day care where they loved him. It was run by a woman named Connie who lived up the street. She would pick up ten or twelve kids every day and take them to a storefront where they would just spend the day. Lin-Manuel was the only child there who could read, so the other children would sit around while he read stories to them. He became the teacher's helper at the grand old age of four. I thought he was wasting a year of learning and often verbalized my feelings. I realize now that I sounded just like my mother when I spent a year at home. But Lin-Manuel loved that little place.

We did not have much support from Luz's family in those early years, but we did have a network of friends who adored us and whom we adored. We would see Luz's family for Thanksgiving and Christmas and not much more. I was clear that Luz could see them whenever she wanted, and my relationship with Cita was solid, so I didn't mind if she spent a few days with her grandmother. But later on, I encouraged a deeper relationship. I remember having a great time growing up in a house where there were always so many people. I always wanted my children to have cousins, and there were many cousins on Luz's side of the family. My sister didn't have children, and my brother was in Puerto Rico with much younger kids. By the time they were teenagers, Cita and Lin-Manuel would spend at least a week each year with the family in New Jersey. They would spend a month in Puerto Rico with my parents. To this day, when Lin-Manuel goes to Austria to spend time with the family of his wife, Vanessa, he visits his Towns cousin Robby, who now lives in Germany. I left my community behind in Puerto Rico, but that family connectedness has traveled with us to New York and the world beyond.

Our overloaded lives did not stop Luz from raising the issue of having more children. But in my head, we were done. Her pregnancies were high risk, and we had a couple of children already. Why would we chance it? We had a great life with Cita and Lin-Manuel.

———

THAT ALL CHANGED UNEXPECTEDLY WHEN LUZ'S NIECE LANDA got in trouble. She was just nineteen years old, and she was pregnant. Someone she loved and trusted had talked her into taking an international flight with drugs in her luggage. Those were the days of mandatory minimum sentences: she was heading to jail. Luz took control of the situation and mobilized the family to support her niece. I was on the board of the Legal Aid Society and asked them to recommend a lawyer who specialized in drug cases. Their advice to Landa was direct: "You have to do three things. You have to get a job. You have to go to therapy. You have to volunteer in an organization. We need to establish that you have roots in your community."

Luz asked her to come and live with us, which she did in 2001. She followed the lawyer's advice: working part-time at the Hispanic Federation, therapy with a social worker with forensic experience, and volunteering at the Community Association of Progressive Dominicans. At her sentencing, the judge asked if Landa could continue to live with us if she was spared going to jail. Of course we said yes. So our niece was sentenced to live with us, abiding by a curfew that still allowed her to work and study. By the second year, she was doing so well that her probation officer recommended that the curfew be lifted. The court agreed.

Miguel was born in 2001, and I took it upon myself to lead the charge for him. It was clear that he had some executive function issues and needed additional support. Even though his mother was present and we always consulted with her, I was the one who carried him around and took him to school. By the time he was four years old, I told Landa that it was very difficult to be in charge of Miguel's education without having any legal rights. We agreed that she and I would both be his legal guardians.

Finding the right school for him was not easy. When we went to our zoned school, the teacher gave us her frank opinion. "I'm a good teacher," she said. "You don't want to send your kid here. This is not the right place for him." We hired a lawyer to ask for alternative placement, which you can do in New York. Eventually we found a place for him at a small private school on the Upper West Side called West End Day School. It had six kids per classroom, along with a teacher and assistant teacher as well as specialists for reading and occupational therapy. Many of the children had some version of attention deficit disorder. It was a nice little school with a very, very strong mental health component— including a psychiatrist and social workers. It was the perfect school for Miguel, and to this day, it's a place he visits.

Miguel was a happy child: very sweet and in your face. But he had difficulty making real friends once he left elementary school. When he transferred to middle school, he missed the small, nurturing environment and found himself in a bigger place where he did well but felt isolated. York Prep was a great school for him, and the staff there are relentless at getting their kids into college, whether they are regular students or have different learning styles. They helped him go to Skidmore College, where he made good friends. He enjoyed his freedom and the whole experience, despite feeling a little tortured by his sense that the world is a big, mean place.

It was tough for us to return to parenting. Miguel required a level of care that our other two children hadn't needed. But he also arrived in my life at a time when we enjoyed a level of flexibility that we never had before: when our finances were beginning to turn around and our adult children required less of our time. I owned my own company and could drive him to school every day.

I believe I was a better parent to Miguel and was more present in his life than I was to Cita and Lin-Manuel. They are his godparents, by design. I wanted some buy-in from our children, some commitment to this new sibling they were getting, which was a quite complicated situation. I believe it worked, and today they have a good relationship with Miguel.

Landa continued to live with us in our house until she finished college a few years ago and got her own apartment. We often disagreed about parenting Miguel. Half the time, she just gave up because sometimes it's not worth fighting with me. The other half, we found a way to move forward.

We took in an extra kid when we thought we were done with raising children. We had some difficult times in an unplanned coparenting situation, but that comes with the territory. Not all of Miguel's stories are for me to tell, but I did my best to get him whatever he needed. No different from what I did with Cita, when all of a sudden I became a parent, or with Lin-Manuel in a more conventional way. In all these parenting situations, one thing is clear: being a dad is my most important job.

———

AROUND THE TIME MIGUEL CAME INTO OUR LIVES, WE TOOK ON the scariest political fight on the issue that meant so much to us as a family: educational opportunity. When we bought our home in Inwood, we had no extra money to send Cita to a private school. Everything was unaffordable. So we began our fight in the parents' movement to improve the schools in our district, which were scoring last in math and reading in the entire city. Looking for educational alternatives for our children was a big deal. Soon we helped create a magnet school, Mott Hall, which was where Cita went for seventh and eighth grades.

At the time, the charter school debate was at its height, and the new charter schools were seen as an instrument of the rich to destroy public education. Hedge funds were getting into education, and the debate was already poisonous. But in my head, the charter movement was not a Republican thing. After all,

President Clinton supported it. I thought that if we created public educational alternatives to which working-class parents could have access, we could create a bit of competition within the public sector—which was never a bad thing. It's one of the reasons I evolved from being a socialist to a capitalist: competition leads to a better product. We also needed to create local boards to be in charge of the schools, which I had been fighting for.

I had no idea I was walking into such a minefield. On one hand, I quickly learned that the unions were against the idea, reasoning that if I send my kid to a charter school, the money that is attached to my child leaves the public school. On the other hand, I did not want kids to be pawns in a political fight. There was an entire generation of kids who were not learning in many schools throughout the city.

My relationship with Roberto Ramírez, who has been my business partner for twenty-five years, was key to approving charter schools in New York. He was an influential young upcoming political figure who also led the Bronx Democratic Party. He took a chance on our concept, and I once again found that fighting from the inside can lead to results.

I wanted to do something different: to create a dual-language charter school and to bring along the UFT, the largest teachers' union in New York City.

Creating the Amber Charter School was intense because the politics were fierce. I understood why. A lot of what the critics said was not wrong, as history has proved. Eva Moskowitz, who started the Success Academy, runs good schools. But critics say that they leave out kids with special needs. They suck resources out of the public system by mandating that they have to be given space. We took a different path with Amber: we purchased all of our own space.

Amber was the first Latino-led community charter school in New York, and one of the few with a UFT chapter. I convinced my friend Michael Stolper to join the board, and for years he has been negotiating contracts for the school. There were four hundred kids whose educational future depended on us doing a good job. I would come home every day with the fear that we might be screwing up the education of those four hundred kids, like the public schools in our district. For twelve years, I was chair of the school, trying to obtain additional resources, trying to hire good people, trying to negotiate with the teachers' unions. I saw those kids. Their future depended on us spending resources, having the right mix of teachers, creating the right curriculum. I went through three executive directors before we found Dr. Vasthi Acosta. She worried about the same things I did and worked relentlessly for the children. We fought with the regulators, but they pushed us to be better. They understood our challenges: how do you meet their standards while also teaching kids with special needs and those who speak less English? What are the educational tools that you need to get the students where they need to go?

It was not easy to own our school buildings, thus avoiding a fight with the Board of Education to get space. In those early days, we needed to obtain a loan to purchase the space, but the loans would run for seven years. The challenge was that a charter ran for only five years. We could be closed two years before the loan ended. So the lender required a guarantor, and I had no choice. I guaranteed the loan with my house—without telling my wife.

Luz eventually found out when I finally stepped down as chair of the board. The incoming board chair, Soledad Hiciano, gave a toast and thanked me for putting up our home as collateral for the school to get its first building. When we got into the car to go home, Luz asked, "What did she mean?"

"Honey, it was so long ago that I don't know what she meant."

"Did you sign anything?" Luz asked.

"I sign many things in the course of my life."

She knew the truth: that I had put up our house as collateral for the school. I hadn't told her because I believed in our gambles. I also knew that everything would work out, and I could live with less agita.

Now Amber Charter is a system of three schools, doing great teaching of Black and Brown kids in our neighborhoods. We were not, as people often said, the hedge-fund alternative to public education. We were the working-class response to developing our public schools. We were not trying to destroy the public education system. We wanted to do better for our community.

Amber was one more resource to develop in my quest to create alternatives for working-class and disadvantaged neighbors—for the immigrants who came to this country to make sure their kids could build a better life.

CHAPTER 5

City Hall

FIGHTS FIND ME. I DON'T FIND FIGHTS. AT LEAST, THAT'S WHAT I tell myself. And the fight over the new schools chancellor in 1985 was an epic one. Many in our community of educational activists were outraged that Robert Wagner Jr., the son of the former mayor, was in line to take the job. He had no direct educational experience, and I thought he would be a disaster. So we started promoting Tony Alvarado, a schools superintendent in East Harlem and, if selected, the first Latino to be chancellor. I did not know him personally, but someone asked me to help him prep for a scheduled debate among the chancellor candidates. When he won the job, he tapped me to be the head of new initiatives—a central part of his promise to reform schools across the city. However, Tony did not survive long in the job. He resigned in disgrace when the *New York Times* revealed that he had borrowed money from subordinates to fund his real estate deals. Everyone around him was desperate to avoid being fired by his replacement, Nat Quinones. Nat had risen inside the bureaucracy—he had a good heart and good credentials, but he was not an agent of change. Besides, he was Latino, and I had defended him in the inner circle when Tony had been chancellor and some had wanted him fired. When he took control, he called me into his office and asked me what job I wanted.

"I'm not an educator," I said. "I came into this place because Tony was going to start an educational revolution. You have to maintain the status quo. But I don't want to stay here. Just give me enough time to find a job."

We were spending the weekend in the Catskills with one of our best friends when the idea of taking a prominent role at City Hall emerged. Our host was Lorraine Cortés-Vázquez, who was a director of programs at the Department for the Aging, and she told me that a job was opening up soon: special adviser to the mayor for Hispanic affairs.

"Oh my God, no," I said. "That's a ceremonial position. All the adviser does is give proclamations throughout this city. I wouldn't take that shitty job."

Lorraine was unfazed. "Jobs are whatever you make them," she said. "You could get that job, and if you see that it's shit, you could always leave."

It was 1987, and Ed Koch had just won reelection with 80 percent of the Latino vote. It was a ridiculous number and such an important part of his winning coalition that he promised to create a Hispanic Commission to see what more he could do for the community. I knew the first deputy mayor, Stan Brezenoff, from my work at the Department of Employment. Stan's career had taken off as he moved from one big city job to another. So I called him up and asked him what he thought. Stan said he thought I would be fantastic for the job, so I put myself forward.

Of course, my struggles in Washington Heights had left some scars, and the local UFT chapter opposed my appointment. They spread the notion that I was anti-Jewish in an attempt to derail me, but my relationships with leaders in my own district suggested the opposite. Stan Michels, my councilman, had become a good friend. We would shoot the breeze and talk about the medieval tapestries he wanted to repair at the Cloisters museum, an extraordinary part of the Metropolitan Museum of Art in Washington Heights. I know more about those tapestries than anyone rightly should. Stan went to Mayor Koch and gave me a ringing endorsement. "Mr. Mayor, there's no one more Jewish than me," he said. "Luis Miranda is not anti-Jewish. He's a friend of the Jewish community, and we would love to have him in that position."

I walked into my interview with Ed Koch with something of an attitude. I told him about all the issues where I disagreed with him. There were plenty. I disagreed with how slowly the housing program was moving. I disagreed with his decision to appoint Wagner to the Board of Education, which made me think he was not really interested in education. I disagreed with his position on hospitals in our communities. And I wanted to see the nine schools built in our district.

"Listen, we got an entire book on everything that needs to happen in the Latino community," he said. "I have appointed Jeremy Travis, one of my assistants to take the lead. You should work with him. A lot of the stuff that you're talking about is going to be taken care of. But when you're out there, you're supporting my policies. You work for me."

I never thought they would offer me the job, but they did. And I quickly changed the job from the guy who delivered proclamations to the guy who helped Ed Koch navigate the Latino community. I would send my staff to do the proclamations, while I would travel the city and report back to Koch to tell him how to mobilize his support in the community. Corruption scandals were beginning to flourish at City Hall, and even though Koch was not involved in them, they were damaging.

Radio and print media, to this day, are important for Latino voters. So we started doing Spanish radio programs every month, and I would be the interpreter. One of the New York newspapers wrote about how the mayor sounded better in Spanish because I would correct his mistakes in the translation. We started writing columns for Spanish newspapers, including *El Diario*. I spent a good deal of time with Koch and went out to lunch with him regularly.

I loved how freely he shared what he thought about anything. Reporters would stop him, and he would give interviews on the spot. I remember one time he started a response by saying, "I really don't know anything about that, but I believe . . . " Only Ed Koch would admit his ignorance before editorializing about something he didn't even know.

Another time, he said the United States should bomb Medellín in Colombia to attack the drug cartels. That was just after the mayor of Bogotá, Andrés Pastrana Arango, came to visit. Koch's comments snowballed into an international incident: the mayor of New York was asking the US military to bomb Medellín. To help clean up the mess, I was asked to put together a conference of mayors from Latin American cities to discuss how to deal with drug trafficking. First, I knew nothing about drug trafficking. Second, why was I in the middle of this international mess? Because I was the special adviser for Hispanic affairs. So we put the conference together, with a dozen mayors from bigger cities across Latin America. And of course, we invited the mayors of Bogotá and Medellín. Despite Koch's inflammatory comments, they all wanted to come to New York to be wined and dined. New York City has an unbelievable appeal for people all over the world. Koch apologized for his comments and explained that when he talked about bombing these places, he really just meant that he wanted them to be cleaned up. Naturally, all the mayors agreed that their cities needed to be cleaned up.

When the conference was over, the mayor of Bogotá gave me a pair of gold cuff links in the shape of coffee beans. I told him that as a public employee, I couldn't accept them, as beautiful as they were. I gave them back to him. After we lost the election in 1989 and left City Hall, he mailed them to me with a lovely note: "You're not a public employee anymore. You can accept them now."

I managed to extract a more lasting benefit from the incident: the introduction of reforms of the police department, which were part of the Hispanic Commission's recommendations. My position did not allow me any access to the NYPD, but Koch's comments, and my planning the conference, opened the door. I told Koch we needed to increase the number of Latinos in the police department because it would take a while for people to move through the ranks. If we did not start recruiting Latino police officers, the NYPD would continue to be all white. I was a little ahead of the times. It was the 1980s, and what is now a widely accepted practice appeared radical back then. The police commissioner Ben Ward, who was the first African American to get the job, was not impressed by this little Latino shrimp coming to tell him how to run his department. As nice as I seem, I was—and continue to be—relentless. I don't back down. I try to work with people, but if I can't, I throw an elbow and see where it lands. To his eternal credit, Ben Ward favored real changes, and we became great friends. We were on the same team, and we all wanted the NYPD to look like New York City. If the department was performing poorly, the whole team looked bad. So we started giving classes for the police test, and today around one-third of the force is Latino—and the first Latino police commissioner was recently appointed.

———

MY OLD FRIENDS ON THE LEFT ACCUSED ME OF SELLING OUT, BUT I quickly realized that this was a golden opportunity to finish the work we had started in Washington Heights. Mayor Koch made the commitment to build the nine schools we wanted; I worked with others in the administration to find the sites and began that process. I had already dealt with the first deputy mayor and the new schools chancellor. Now I could keep an eye on things until the schools were built. I would receive updates on how the construction was going. I was also fortunate that there was a blueprint of what the Latino community needed from government, drawn from a series of hearings that the Hispanic Commission had held across the city. There was a $10 billion housing plan that included the renovations of tens of thousands of affordable homes. One day, Koch and I were in the Bronx, and he asked if I wanted to see something. We drove along the Grand Concourse as he showed me how every vacant building was being turned into affordable housing.

"Shouldn't we have bilingual signs outside telling people where to call for the lottery?" I asked. "How does that happen?"

Koch admitted he didn't know, and he promptly got the housing commissioner to do just that. Soon there were bilingual signs with phone numbers telling people what they needed to do to get in line to secure one of these apartments. It was real affordable housing—not the bullshit that sometimes passes for affordable housing today.

This was the chance to get a lot of shit done, which was why I didn't mind being on the inside. In fact, it helped me develop my thick skin. My father used to say, "Al palo que pare mangos, le tiran piedras"—a saying about mango trees that roughly translates as "The more productive you are, the more you become a target." At the time, the editor of *El Diario*, which was a very influential newspaper, decided to hate me. He had loved my work as a community activist, organizing the Dominican parents who were his readers. But he turned on me when I moved into City Hall. He actually met with Mayor Koch and told him that he would stop criticizing Koch in the paper if the mayor appointed him to something. He also insisted that he didn't want me in that meeting. Koch told me afterward that he would not cross that line. "I don't mind doing political deals," he said. "But this is extortion."

We made huge strides for the Latino community during those years, thanks to an unlikely source: Ronald Reagan. We opposed everything that Reagan stood for except his landmark immigration reform legislation in 1986. I hated Reagan, and I couldn't believe he had signed the law. The law made it illegal to hire undocumented immigrants, but it also gave amnesty to anyone who had arrived in the country without official paperwork before 1982. Almost three million immigrants were granted permanent residency as a result, and the law remains—after all these years—the last big immigration reform this country managed to pass in more than forty years.

I saw the impact it had on real people who were able to come out of the shadows, whose families were finally legal citizens. I had met so many parents without documents in my school board fights. I knew how difficult it was to get them even to register for a school board election. Amnesty had a real impact on entire communities across the city and the country. I remember people coming to tell me proudly they had received a social security number. It was life-changing.

At the end of the day, you have to keep in mind that you do all this work for a reason, not just for power. I have met many people who have forgotten that power is intoxicating, and they feel like that's a big enough reason to do these jobs. But I never forgot, and never do, that you commit to this work because there is some bigger impact that you can help bring to the world. That amnesty law was an early and vivid lesson in helping to deliver something much bigger and better to the real world.

Koch and I had regular lunches together every couple of weeks, and most of the stuff that happens in government took place in those informal lunches. At one of them, Ed told me to make the amnesty program a success in New York. When I complained that the legislation had no money attached to it, he told me to work with Roger Alvarez, who led the community development agency. The agency received block grants from the federal government, so it always had resources. Initially, Alvarez's team denied that they had any money, but it was soon clear that if I had a specific project to support, they could find the money. They funded everything we needed. We would go all over the city, talking to different community groups every night. These groups needed money to help process all of the amnesty applications. The massive undertaking helped build great relationships with the Ecuadorian, Colombian, and Dominican communities. It also helped build my team from four employees to seventeen. I kept asking Koch's chief of staff, Diane Coffey, for more people, and she kept giving me more.

The job was not entirely about substantive policy initiatives. I dealt with plenty of nonsense. Among the Dominican community, there were two factions of leadership struggling over a Dominican parade. Parades are big-money propositions, and I was asked—as the mayor's Hispanic adviser—to mediate between the two. One day I was meeting with Koch in his office when I told him I needed to go sit down with the rival factions in my neighborhood.

"I need to get there before anybody else to make sure nobody has guns or knives," I told him, half joking and half serious. Koch looked puzzled.

"Hyperbole?" he asked.

"No. No hyperbole."

"You shouldn't be there," he told me.

"I live there, Mayor. This is literally three blocks from my house."

"No," he insisted. "You got to go with police."

"Are you crazy? I'm going to show up to my neighborhood with police? It doesn't make any sense."

"Then you need undercovers," he replied.

I had been meeting with these groups for weeks. I wasn't suddenly in need of protection, and I told him so. Still, he insisted on having his security drive me over, and I convinced them to stay outside.

Koch ran for an unprecedented fourth term in 1989, and we all knew the odds were against us. The scandals were overwhelming. Party bosses in the Bronx and Brooklyn had been indicted and convicted for bribery and extortion, giving contracts to companies they created. The transportation department was at the center of much of it. Koch survived the scandals but not the election.

Besides, I read the papers. There was a real movement for the city to elect its first Black mayor, not least because racial tensions were running high after several racist murders. David Dinkins was able to put together a strong coalition of good government groups and minorities. By the time of the primaries, we received maybe one out of every ten Black votes. The only people solidly behind Koch continued to be the Jewish community.

I continued to see Ed regularly for lunch on Saturdays. Whenever we went out, people would come up to him and say, "I voted for you." He had no problem telling them they were lying.

"If everyone I see on the streets who says they voted for me actually voted for me, I would be mayor," he used to say. "You didn't vote for me."

I am proud of my work in the Koch administration. In our very first meeting, he told me that if I agreed with him on six out of ten things and stayed quiet on the other four—to debate them privately—then we could work together. He was true to his word, and I was true to mine.

———

As the Koch administration wound down, I had a clear sense of how much I was willing to compromise my principles to achieve results—results that would otherwise take years of pressure from the outside. I also had a much better sense of what I was not prepared to compromise on and how elastic my belief system really was. I had worked closely with one of the biggest political figures in the United States, perhaps second only to the president, and we had achieved tangible accomplishments for Latinos and for New York City.

I also knew that I wasn't a career bureaucrat. I wanted to work in places where I could make real changes. Everyone was telling me to stay on with Dinkins and go into a line agency, delivering services to New Yorkers. But I was leaving a job that had a lot of influence and power, and I didn't see myself working in one of the agencies. Instead, I spent a lot of time placing all the people I had hired in good positions so they could continue to use their talents in government. As for me, I was too high profile to hide out somewhere. I knew how power worked and that I needed to pack my bags.

The owner of Mega radio station, Raúlito Alarcón, asked me if I wanted to work there until I figured out my next move. Mega and Amor were the top two Spanish radio stations in the city. I knew nothing about radio, but I did know how to talk. It sounded like an interesting thing to do. They gave me the freedom to do whatever I wanted, so I started two public affairs programs that I still do every week, over three decades later. Soon I took over the bureaucratic tasks, like the regulatory need for FCC reporting. And because my portfolio was not big enough, I started getting up every morning at 4:00 a.m. to help put together the news from 5:00 to 9:00. The news director could use my help. It was a complete change, but it had an enormous influence on what Latinos heard every morning in the city.

I made sure that sports and entertainment were not the only news, even if they grabbed listeners' attention. I made sure that local elected officials doing good work were mentioned. We also highlighted the work of local groups. Then, in my local affairs programs, I interviewed the movers and shakers in politics, community development, and government. Radio taught me to be brief and to develop cogent arguments in a couple of minutes—because if not, there was another station with music on.

As Koch's final days in office came to an end, he asked me if I wanted to serve on any city boards. Because of my training as a psychologist a decade earlier, I suggested the mental health department. On almost his last day, he called me into his office to tell me I should call the head of Health + Hospitals. I was confused and reminded him that I had talked about mental health.

"Well, I misunderstood," he said. "You are now a member of the Health + Hospitals corporation board. Good luck."

It was too late to fix the error. While they both had the word "health" in their names, they were not at all the same. The Health + Hospitals corporation in New York City is the largest public health care system in the United States, serving more than a million patients every year. That was how another unplanned adventure started.

At the Health + Hospitals corporation, I built a reputation as an independent thinker and a hardworking board member. I knew absolutely nothing about hospitals, but I was willing to put in the time to learn about them. I took on Dinkins whenever he did something I thought was wrong, but the chairman was a Dinkins appointee, and he knew that—even if I was a critic at times—I would be supportive if he really needed me. What I had learned about the process of building schools became helpful. I was made chair of the capital committee as we were building all over the system. I had gotten to know the system pretty well and would grill people in detail every time they presented to us. I hated the careless way people treated public dollars simply because the money was not theirs.

When Rudy Giuliani took over the city four years later, an old friend, Ninfa Segarra, became his deputy mayor. She had been a Dinkins appointee at the Board of Education but had soured on him and supported Giuliani. I stayed close to her because she was one of the few Latinos close to Giuliani, and I thought someone should help her out. When Giuliani won, he asked me to run the Health + Hospitals corporation. I declined at first, but Ninfa insisted that I should meet with him, so I did.

"I really want you to do this," he told me. "What will it take?"

I told him I would do the job, but I would be critical of his administration, just as I had been critical of Dinkins. The moment the job contradicted my values, I would leave. "Is that something this administration can live with?" I asked. He said yes and chose me as a token Democrat to chair the Health + Hospitals board.

I figured I would see what I could do. However, I learned early on that Giuliani was mean to his core. I had few interactions with him, but one day I was in Gracie Mansion during a discussion of the schools chancellor's performance. I witnessed Giuliani making fun of him because he had cried in public. What a creep.

We began to deliver on the promise that we were supposed to take care of poor people in a respectful way, even when people objected. We were criticized heavily for spending $1 million on the lobby of Lincoln Hospital in the Bronx. Nobody says a peep if a private hospital spends that kind of money on marble to make a grand entrance. But people don't think the poor deserve nice places or that you should spend money to make their lives better. I also called out our own poor performance. I halted the renovation of Kings County Hospital in Brooklyn because we were doing such a bad job, wasting resources, even though the place needed it. Board chairs don't typically do that.

A year and a half into the job, I reached the line where my values met the politics of the Giuliani administration. There were many people who told me to ignore the fight and that I could continue to make many changes if I stayed where I was. But it was emotional and important. Governor George Pataki was proposing cuts to the state's HIV/AIDS programs. It was only around $15 million, compared to our total budget of more than $3 billion. The total cuts were not even a rounding error. But it was the middle of the HIV/AIDS epidemic, and it seemed wrong to me to cut any funding at that time. There were other ways to make cuts and realize savings. We were going to move the ambulance system into the fire department, delivering enormous savings. But Giuliani said no. My majority on the board was very slim. I had a margin of just one or two votes because there were so many different appointees from different administrations. I always had to meet with people to convince them about some case to win the votes.

So when the previous board chair, who had stayed on the board, proposed a resolution in 1994 condemning Pataki and Giuliani for cutting HIV/AIDS funding, I called the mayor's office to tell them I would support the resolution.

"Remember when I told you that whenever my work as an advocate was against my work as the chair of Health + Hospitals, I would always be the advocate? This is it," I said. "What you're doing is wrong. I'm not going to support us cutting $15 million in AIDS services."

Giuliani's team said I could not vote against the cut. My father was going into heart surgery that morning, and they suggested that I spend some time with him. The vote was that day, and if I traveled to see my father in Puerto Rico, I would miss it—and the resolution would fail.

"I'm not doing that," I said. "I'm not a surgeon, and there's nothing I can do for my dad other than wait. I can wait in New York and vote for the resolution."

They again told me that I could not support the resolution. So I tendered my resignation.

Did I do the right thing? I had learned during the Koch years that your convictions can be elastic. But this was territory where my convictions held firm. We were in the middle of the epidemic. People were dying left and right. Our hospitals were full of people with AIDS, but there was indifference because of the perception that the only ones getting sick were gay or people using drugs.

I quit my job and went straight to Puerto Rico to see my father anyway.

I figured that if they had let me vote for the resolution, Giuliani might have gotten some credit for allowing me to vote that way. I would have given no interviews, and people would have interpreted it as Giuliani shitting on Pataki, which often happened. Instead, it became an enormous mess because I was resigning over the cuts, and I was being forced out. The Giuliani team didn't care until it was front-page news in the *New York Times*. When the *Times* called, I simply said, "There's nothing to explain. The people of New York didn't elect me. They elected Giuliani, and his policy is to cut AIDS funding. I couldn't support his policy, so I left."

Giuliani began to have a much more contentious relationship with the gay community after that article.

However, there was a lot of good that I wasn't able to do because I was no longer on the inside. That was the trade-off. For instance, when I became chair, we expanded MetroPlus, a low-cost health insurance program that was our managed care program. The world was beginning to change, and Health + Hospitals was in danger of losing its patients to managed care companies. In that world, Health + Hospitals would get paid only as a provider of services. Instead, we wanted to be an insurer as well as a provider for our patients. When you are the insurer, you get paid per patient regardless of whether you provide any services. So I poured money into MetroPlus, including money into advertising so we could compete with the managed care companies that were giving away free toasters to sign up members. When I quit, that initiative was hurt. The system lost a lot of resources as a result.

Principles and values matter. But so does getting shit done. The struggle between the two is not an easy one for anyone who really understands the meaning of public service and the power of government to make life better for people who really need it.

CHAPTER 6

Latinidad

FOR A FEW MONTHS AFTER THE END OF THE KOCH ADMINIS-
tration in 1989, I was doing odd jobs consulting here and
there when I heard about a unique opportunity. United Way of
New York was going to create a series of federations in the mold
of the United Jewish Appeal and the Catholic Charities. There
would be an Asian American Federation, an Associated Black
Charities, and a Hispanic Federation. The goal was to help the
nonprofit sector across the different communities. The federations would raise money for their members and provide technical
services to make individual agencies stronger so they could serve
New Yorkers in need. I loved the challenge and especially the
fact that these organizations didn't already exist. I could create
something entirely new to help all the Latino organizations and

leaders that I had already been working with for more than a decade. I applied for the job and was hired, becoming the founding executive director of the Hispanic Federation.

I was given $300,000 and an eight-page concept paper that I quickly decided was insufficient. So I went to the people I knew who could help create a Latino nonprofit network: the local Ecuadorian and Colombian organizations, the Puerto Rican Family Institute, Aspira, and many other organizations that needed to help create this new federation.

I had known from the very beginning of my journey in New York, and from my time at Aspira, that nonprofits were central to the life of a community. Aspira was committed to developing Puerto Rican leadership. The Hispanic Federation grew out of the concept that our community needed sustainability. It needed the help that the nonprofit sector was delivering. At that point, the sector was a small group of institutions that the Puerto Rican community had created as it moved forward. But when the United Way approached me, the Latino community was already more varied than just Puerto Ricans. I knew that we needed to add to our community, but the institutions were not there. We needed to help create them. I believed we needed to develop more organizations for more communities to deliver for our people and to deliver power. We needed to create leadership.

There were very few non–Puerto Rican institutions. There were some smaller groups out there, like the Centro Civico Colombiano and Alianza Dominicana. But we needed to grow, and we needed to be larger than the sum of our parts. I didn't know if I wanted to be considered Hispanic; I don't even know what that word means. But if gringos, in their Black-and-white binary construction, wanted to understand the world by creating this concept of Hispanic and grouping a whole bunch of people under the same umbrella, then let's go! Instead of being small communities of a million each, let's be three million or thirty million. We weren't even asking for it. They even lumped Asians together, even though they don't all speak the same language or have the same culture. This was because of white people's need to understand the world in a simple way. So we were going to do them a favor. We were now going to speak as thirty million people. It was a game changer. We would use their concept to sit at the table with much more power.

I had no idea whether the United Way of New York had any of those intentions, but it didn't matter. It was the first time I understood that nonprofits could develop power while also serving people who have needs. You could use philanthropic and government dollars to provide services. And then you could go to the mayor alongside thirty other executive directors from all over the city telling him they needed additional funding. When we went to the New York Community Trust, which funds nonprofits, the people there were so flustered. They had good intentions, and they thought—as they all do—that good intentions were enough to placate us. Instead, we looked at all their grantees and told them just 2 percent of their money was going to Latino-led organizations. They were our partner, and they weren't happy. But that was what it meant to consolidate power, to increase resources and services. Our goal was to grab power because power was never going to be given freely. We had to fight for it.

We also needed to expand our giving from our own community. It was 1990, and I didn't know fifty affluent Latinos in New York that I could put in a room and ask how much they would donate. I remember the first time we got a $5,000 donation from an individual. My development director, John Gutierrez, and I were astonished that somebody would give so much money to a group that was basically a concept. It was the first large donation we got, and we invited the donor, Carlos Morales, to join the board. That was one of the main reasons we were created: to raise funding from Latinos.

We stayed the course, developing our first gala. We needed gala chairs, and we were already talking to Oscar de la Renta, the great Dominican fashion designer. We were looking for another when my vice president, Nereida Andino, told me that Bianca Jagger had called twice for me. I told Nereida to call her back, but she said Bianca had insisted on talking to me.

"She's Bianca Jagger," she said.

"Who's Bianca Jagger?" I asked.

"Do you know Mick Jagger?"

"No, I don't."

I was still unimpressed when they explained who Mick Jagger was. Being married to someone famous doesn't make you famous. But everybody told me Bianca Jagger was famous, and I was looking for a gala chair. So we arranged to go to lunch at a small neighborhood Caribbean diner close to our offices on Thirty-Seventh Street. It was one of those places where they have the food already on display, and you just pick what you want and sit down to eat it. Bianca asked for a salad, and I think they just opened up some vegetables from a Del Monte can. She asked what dressing they had, and the Cuban guy behind the counter suggested vinegar, oil, maybe some salt and pepper. She didn't make a fuss about it. But my wife was astonished when I told her afterward: "You took Bianca Jagger there? You're such a peasant." Despite my manners, Bianca became our gala chair.

That was how we began to develop a place that could unite the elite, the corporations, political leaders, and community organizations. We became the place that brought people together.

It was a fantastic experience, building a diverse team of various Latino groups. We started from scratch, creating technical assistance programs for agencies and organizations. They all had different needs. The Centro Civico Colombiano needed to incorporate as a nonprofit volunteer organization. The Puerto Rican Family Institute needed an elevator to make its building wheelchair-accessible. My job was to sell the concept of Hispanics working together under one umbrella at a time when the notion did not exist. It was each of our "tribes"—Dominicans, Puerto Ricans, Ecuadorians, Colombians—moving from the singular to the plural.

We developed a set of criteria for who could become members of the federation. You didn't need to pay, but the organizations needed to meet the following requirements: a majority of Latino directors on the board, servicing a majority-Latino population, and Latino leadership at the executive level. Those three measures are still the criteria today. There were organizations on the cusp of qualifying, such as the Council on Adoptable Children, which was a foster care agency serving a rapidly growing Latino population. They organized a Latino-majority board and hired Latino leadership.

Our role was to help them build their organizations. We didn't have a pot of cash, but we could help them get cash. We quickly developed the technical capabilities to help them grow. I put together a group of proposal writers who were dispatched to the organizations and agencies. All of a sudden, these groups were getting money because they were submitting professional proposals.

My friends helped: Michael Stolper, who is now my compadre, led the group of writers, mostly law students, in preparing proposals. We got lots of pro bono work offers, including auditing firms for these organizations. The work might not have been sexy, but it was substantive: we were developing groups that were building and strengthening our community.

My job involved mostly fundraising and solving problems. Government agencies always had issues with contracts, but I now knew folks in government and could call the commissioner at the Department of Employment, for instance, to say that I knew the National Puerto Rican Forum's numbers weren't great. I had created those indicators when I'd been at the department. But I promised I would assign someone to work with them to improve. That way, organizations avoided defunding.

Sometimes we needed to help create new agencies. That was the core of the Latin American Integration Center, the precursor of Make The Road. Sara Maria Cuchilla, a recent political refugee from Colombia, came to visit me about her idea to create a new institution to help Colombians. I agreed and we moved forward.

I also had to use my powers of persuasion to win over the skeptics who distrusted the whole mission. Carmen Arroyo ran the South Bronx Community Corporation, and she influenced lots of other community leaders. If I could win her over, we would gain credibility, and we could then recruit other organizations. But Carmen was from Puerto Rico, and she wanted to make sure that our collective power did not diminish Puerto Rican power.

"I don't know why you're doing this," she told me. "This is going to dilute Puerto Rican power. Now you're creating this umbrella, and everyone is equal. The Dominicans are going to eat our lunch, with all of these other groups that are rapidly growing."

"Carmen, Carmen, you're going to continue to have the power that you have," I said. "To the extent that we join with others, we'll have more power because of the numbers."

Carmen said she would give me one year to see what happened. For that year, there was nothing that Carmen wanted that Carmen did not get. She soon ran for office in the New York State Assembly and won, becoming the first-ever Puerto Rican woman elected there. I supported her.

We grew very quickly. I went back to the United Way and argued for more money, accusing them of tokenism. I went to the Ford Foundation and told them they should be ashamed of themselves for failing to support our community properly. I had heated arguments with the leadership of the New York Community Trust. To their credit, and despite my abrasive style, they all came through. With their contributions, I created a fund called the CORE Initiative that gave out unsexy grants. People needed to pay for electricity but were three months overdue. People needed an audit. People needed to hire a fundraising staffer. Today, CORE is the largest grant program for Latinos in the city of New York, with support from the city council to the tune of $3 million a year.

For me, the Hispanic Federation is always a work in progress. We didn't have a home, so we got money from the state and the city to buy condo space. I gave my radio programs over to the Hispanic Federation, so they continued as Hispanic Federation programs, not Luis Miranda programs. Even though I left the Federation in 1998, it would forever be part of our family. After Hurricane Maria destroyed so much of Puerto Rico in 2017, we raised millions to help rebuild— money that the Hispanic Federation managed. We spent more than $45 million in Puerto Rico over five years. Some of the money paid for small things, such as an agency audit. Some of the money paid for bigger goals, like the coffee initiative that involved more than one thousand coffee growers and major companies such as Starbucks and Nespresso, with the support of the Rockefeller Foundation and other donors. As a result, local coffee production today is higher than it was the year before Maria hit Puerto Rico.

———

AFTER SIX YEARS BUILDING THE HISPANIC FEDERATION, I WAS beginning to get bored. It had become the center for everything that involved Latino groups in New York. There wasn't an elected official who didn't come to us for help—or to offer help. We had grown into an important political and social force, not just an agency. At some point, I realized that what I really wanted to do was run campaigns: that was my next challenge. I didn't know how to do that for a living because until then, I had been doing it forever and for free.

I talked to people at United Way and the United Jewish Appeal, and they were very helpful. Whenever I had questions, whenever I needed advice, they were there to help. The best advice they gave me was that there was always some turmoil when a leader leaves a place, especially the founding leader. So for the federation to survive, I needed to leave a couple of years of funding in place so that the next director had time to find his or her own footing. By that time I had a successor in mind—Lorraine Cortés-Vázquez. I had convinced my board chair, Mariano Guzmán, that she was a great choice. She was the head of Aspira at that point, and she had city government experience as an assistant commissioner. As a statement, I thought it was good optics for the next leader to be a Dominican–Puerto Rican woman succeeding a Puerto Rican man. The board agreed, and with a couple of years of funding secured, I could leave the federation in a good place. They wanted to give me a plaque with my name on it, but I said no. "If you're going to give me a present, please give me a printer," I said. "That's what I need. I don't need another plaque."

So they gave me a printer. I have always been very practical that way.

For my farewell party, Lin-Manuel created a song about my life at the Hispanic Federation based on the musical *The Capeman*, whose central song is "Born in Puerto Rico." He was eighteen years old and ready to start a career in film or performing and writing—screenplays, music, poems. He was always very creative, and his performance at my farewell party was epic.

In contrast, Cita had already finished college and was very clear about what she wanted to do. She was going to work for a couple of years, then do her MBA at NYU Stern or Columbia, then get herself a boyfriend, get married at thirty, and have three children by the age of thirty-five. She did all of that, by the way, on her timeline.

I, on the other hand, found myself at a new crossroads. I was forty-four years old and knew that I only wanted to run campaigns. It was less a midlife crisis than a purpose crisis. Everything I did had a purpose. I had raised money for causes and institutions for so long, but now I was about to go into business for myself. It was something I hadn't done since selling records as a teenager. I would be creating my own schedule, on my own time, with no idea whether this would work. I had a printer from the Hispanic Federation and a promise of some consulting work for a year. United Way agreed to be a client too, so there was a foundation upon which to build.

My real break came from someone I had met through the Health + Hospitals corporation. Carol Raphael was head of the Visiting Nurse Services, and she had been surprised by my principled resignation from the board. She called me out of the blue to give me a special project to develop. Almost half her clients were Latinos, and she needed help to make the organization Hispanic-friendly. The work involved taking a close look at her organization and figuring out how to infuse Latinidad—our shared Latino culture, experience, and identity—into protocols and written materials. The organization started basic Spanish classes for the nurses. There was no way they would be able to hire enough bilingual nurses, but they could at least place phone callers on hold in Spanish. Simple things could add up to make a big difference. They were a client for a long time, and their support allowed me to hire my one employee, Tony Reyes, who had worked with me at the Federation. It was not campaign work, but it allowed me to build a company and start the work that I wanted to do.

———

I HAD EXPERIENCED MY FIRST CAMPAIGN MANY YEARS EARLIER, AS a volunteer. It was 1982, and redistricting had just happened. A congressional district had been created in East New York that was more than 50 percent Latino, and Jack John Olivero decided to run. There was only one Latino member of Congress at the time: Robert García from the Bronx. So this would have been a historic campaign. Olivero was a former AT&T executive who was board chair of the Community Service Society, the oldest nonprofit in the city. He was also one of the architects of the Puerto Rican Legal Defense Fund and had fought successfully for bilingual education and against racism. I was approached to volunteer simply because I worked in Williamsburg, but I soon ended up running the campaign at the age of twenty-eight.

With some professional support that Jack had secured, we gathered our petitions to qualify him for the ballot and defend him against the

Brooklyn Democratic machine that was fielding its own candidate, Ed Towns (who was no relation to my wife). We also fended off a local Latino candidate who was encouraged to run to split the Latino vote. We lost with 25 percent of the vote, while the other Puerto Rican candidate got 24 percent. The Democratic machine knew what it was doing: it split the vote to win. I learned a valuable lesson that I cherished for a while: try to be the only Latino candidate in a race.

As it turned out, that election changed my life because it was there that I first met Roberto Ramírez, the man who would become my close friend and business partner. In 1982, Roberto came into our district with a whole contingent from the Bronx to help with the campaign. After the election, Roberto and I stayed in touch. A couple of years later, he was running for the New York assembly and called to ask me to donate to his campaign. I gave money, and I also volunteered a couple of times. They were trying to get an opponent off the ballot, and I knew something about the mechanics of that. In the days before computers, you could use a technique called Signed Another Petition (SAP). You could get rid of lots of signatures by looking for SAPs. Roberto also asked me to help on election day, which I was happy to do. He lost the campaign, but we remained friends.

Roberto was a lawyer, born in Puerto Rico in a little town on the west coast. He had arrived in New York as an eighteen-year-old, and his circumstances were challenging. He worked as a janitor and ran an adult education program to make a living. He was one of the brightest people I had ever met. He possessed raw intelligence and also worked his ass off. He was elected to the state assembly during his second year of law school at NYU. He is stubborn and driven, but he has incredible insight that helps him understand situations. He likes to say that politics is the perfect combination of science and magic—if you apply the science, the magic may happen. I tend to look at the science of the polling data. He prefers to look at the magic of campaigning. We made a great team.

Early on, Roberto surrounded himself with advisers—his kitchen cabinet. Half of the people in this group were loyal and hardworking but average. They would often say yes to what Roberto wanted. I was not one of them. I don't know why you would want people who yes you to death rather than challenge you to be better. The more we became friends, the more he realized that I would always tell him the truth and challenge him. He eventually won his seat in the state assembly, representing the Bronx for a decade and rising to become chairman of the Democratic Party in the borough. When I was chair of the Health + Hospitals corporation, he was the chair of the urban health subcommittee of the state assembly, and he held considerable power. We would fight all the time when his committee passed some law that would cost us millions of dollars without giving us any more money.

"You are great at passing fucking regulations because you don't have to implement them and make them work," I would tell him. "I have to run a system every single day with thirty thousand employees."

"Well, let's figure out how I could get you some additional money," he would say.

"No, I'm just going to go to the Senate, which thank God is controlled by Republicans and not by you guys," I bluffed. "I'll kill it at the Senate level. Or I'll go to the governor, and he will have more sense than you."

Once again, my pronouncements are often made just to rattle people. I never got help from the Republicans. Roberto always came through with additional funds.

———

A FUN BUT CHALLENGING CONTEST I LED WAS TO ELECT GUILL-ermo Linares to the city council in 1992, a decade after Jack's congressional race. A district had once again been created that could plausibly elect Latino leadership. Our competition included Maria Luna, a district leader of the Democratic Party who had the support of the local party establishment, and Adriano Espaillat, a political insurgent who had created a Democratic club in the area. Both Adriano and Guillermo ran grassroots campaigns.

Linares, like his Latino opponents, was born in the Dominican Republic. He had arrived in New York as a teenager and grown up in the Bronx. He had worked as a taxi driver to pay for college, becoming a citizen while studying. He was warm, low-key, smart, and very down-to-earth. We always used to say that he couldn't walk two blocks without stopping twenty times to talk to people. And he would have full conversations with them, without regard to the schedule he had to follow. Whereas Espaillat was more politically astute, Linares found it difficult to prioritize his attention. He treated every single person he met like the most important person. He was the best human being, even if he wasn't the best politician. People liked him.

We had already organized thousands of parents for the school board elections in the preceding years. By this time, six years after the amnesty, many were becoming citizens and could vote. Our campaign had very little money, but we didn't really need money. We had troops. I'm not sure we even did a single mailing. We had lots of street literature, and we were in every single school every day. We had cadres of people in every school and could assemble fifty or seventy-five people in a nanosecond. I knew how many people we had registered in each school, where to collect signatures, and which subway stations were the best to contact voters.

People continued to question why I, as a proud Puerto Rican, was working to elect a Dominican representative. They were tough times. I had learned from the Hispanic Federation that the most important personal attribute for Latinos was not the notion of being Hispanic; it was their country of origin that defined them. Most of them considered themselves Puerto Rican first, or Dominican first, or Colombian first. They were Latino second. At the same time, the only way I knew for us to share power was to gain power in the first place. Here was a chance to elect the first of their group to a visible public office—not just in New York but across the United States. I jumped at the chance. After the 1990 census, this district was created to try to elect a Dominican representative, as Dominicans were the overwhelming majority there. They worked hard, and I could help them. I wanted to be part of something that I thought was a necessary step in the development of our community: to begin to elect Latinos from various countries of origin.

It was a hard-fought but respectful campaign. Politics were very different in those days, before the culture deteriorated to where it is today. During the campaign, Espaillat's father became sick. When we learned about it, we all went to the hospital. We were all concerned that he was going through that family crisis. And when his father died, we all went to the funeral as if he had been the father of our own candidate.

On election night, the results came in from our own staffers in every corner of the district. We taught people how to close a polling place and come to headquarters with the numbers for each election district. We added them all up ourselves, and we knew the results that night. We had won a historic victory. Guillermo called his opponents, and they quickly conceded because they were also counting the votes for themselves.

Years later, I would take the lead in helping elect Adriano Espaillat as the first Dominican-American to Congress. Twice we came close to defeating Charlie Rangel, the powerful congressperson from Harlem. When he announced his retirement, we finally won.

SIX YEARS LATER, ROBERTO AND I SPENT THE WEEKEND together at a place my family had bought in Montauk, at the eastern end of Long Island. Our plan was to talk about the future. Roberto wanted to quit being chair of the Bronx Democratic Party, but I argued that he needed to stay in place to save the Bronx from political implosion. We had dreams of electing a Puerto Rican mayor. I would start a consulting company and then run the mayoral campaign for our friend Freddy Ferrer in 2001. Roberto would leave the assembly in 2000, and we would go into business together.

Fernando "Freddy" Ferrer was the most prominent Latino official in New York City. Raised by Puerto Rican parents in the Bronx, he had been part of Aspira, as had I. Before running for mayor, he had already served on the city council for years before rising to become Bronx borough president. He was more than just a credible candidate for mayor: he was a realistic prospect to become the first Latino mayor of New York. I was totally committed to his campaign, which almost bankrupted me because I couldn't work on any other client projects while I worked so hard to elect the first Puerto Rican mayor of the city I loved.

There was a real path to victory. We knew that we needed to overperform among Latino voters—not just among Puerto Ricans but across the community—to compensate for our underrepresentation among registered voters overall. We also knew that we needed to build a coalition with African Americans that had not existed since 1989, when Latino voters had supported David Dinkins. That had been more than a decade earlier. We didn't know whether Black voters would support a Latino candidate the way Latinos had supported Dinkins. On top of all that, we needed about 20 percent of the white vote to win the primary.

We worked hard to convince Dominicans that Freddy as a Puerto Rican would represent them and develop a piece of Latinidad unity. I had some influence with Dominican leaders because of my work to get Guillermo Linares elected. Statistically, Latinos voted less in primaries. So our strategy focused on identifying and convincing previous Latino voters—especially those who had voted for Hillary Clinton in her Senate race—to come out for the primary. With few resources, it felt like a better strategy than trying to convince non-voters to come out for the first time or registering new voters.

We were campaigning nonstop when Roberto, who was a big political figure in our campaign, decided to go to Vieques. For Puerto Ricans, Vieques was the number one issue at the time because the military base on the island was still being used for weapons target practice by the US Navy. When a civilian employee was killed by a bomb, the protests against the navy's presence began in earnest. Roberto felt compelled to take the risk of going to Vieques because he was committed to fighting against the bombing of the island. I remember telling him not to trespass on military land; otherwise, he would get arrested. Regardless, he trespassed and was arrested.

I learned of his arrest when he called me from a boat as he was being transported to a penitentiary to spend the next forty days in jail, along with Rev. Al Sharpton; José Rivera, a state assemblyman from the Bronx; and New York City Council member Adolfo Carrión.

All of a sudden, I was in charge of Freddy's campaign. We organized a picket in front of the penitentiary in Brooklyn every day, while Roberto and his fellow protesters decided to go on a hunger strike. I was torn between feeling angry that I was running the campaign—when I had told Roberto not to trespass—and intense disappointment. Roberto was normally so disciplined, and this was really out of character for him. Still, we pivoted toward a Vieques campaign and used the fight as a rallying cry for Puerto Rican votes and for Freddy in New York. It turned out to be very successful. I even traveled to Vieques with Freddy, although he promised not to go to jail. Meanwhile, Roberto and Al Sharpton became great friends in jail. When they were released, in mid-August, Sharpton promised his support for Freddy, and so did most of the Black leadership in the city. Was that the science or magic of politics? Either way, Roberto had succeeded.

Just a couple of weeks before the election, we were in a great position. But in a multicandidate race, it was hard to land a knockout blow. Our biggest rival was Mark Green, who had served most recently as the city's public advocate.

I'd never liked Mark Green. I didn't know him personally, and he'd never done anything to me, but he always came across as an asshole. Green had been groomed to become mayor for two decades by a wealthy family and the Democratic establishment, and he acted like it. Freddy, on the other hand, was unknown to the white establishment because the Bronx was considered the outer boroughs. I took a call from a veteran *New York Times* reporter, Joyce Purnick, whom I knew from my days in City Hall. She wanted to meet because, as she explained, "Freddy Ferrer may be the next mayor, and I don't know him."

Primary day was the second Tuesday in September, and we felt good about our chances. It was a perfect fall day, with a clear blue sky across the city: September 11, 2001. I had arrived at our office on Houston and Broadway early, around 5:00 a.m. By 8:00, we had deployed volunteers throughout the city. Then the unimaginable happened. From our vantage point, we could see all the way downtown to the World Trade Center as the smoke billowed out of one of the towers. At first we all thought it was an accident. I went downstairs with Michael Stolper and bought a coffee. We talked about what it might mean if the election was delayed as the sirens screamed all around us. When we returned to our office, we saw the explosion after the second plane struck the second tower. Then we heard the news about the Pentagon.

There was pandemonium at the campaign. People started freaking out as we began to understand that the country was under attack. It wasn't some random plane that had missed the airport runway. Campaign staff began crying, and many wanted to go home.

Fifteen minutes after the second tower was hit at 9:03 a.m., the police banged on the door of our offices, insisting that we evacuate. But we were in the middle of an election, and I couldn't leave my position in the heart of it all, even as ambulances and fire trucks raced down Broadway.

"I can't evacuate until the election is canceled," I told the officer, who reluctantly allowed a couple of us to stay behind. One team member came to me and said, "I know you're looking for volunteers. I'll stay. I'm here in New York alone, and I know nothing is going to happen." I asked another kid who was from Texas, living alone in the city, if he minded staying. I got a few more volunteers to stay behind, but it didn't make much difference.

It was hard to get anyone on the phone because the lines were down. I tried to call Luz but couldn't get through. Eventually I got hold of her and said I needed to stay in the office to run the campaign. "You do what you need to do," she said calmly.

Lin-Manuel was at school at Wesleyan in Connecticut, desperately trying to get hold of us. He finally connected via Instant Messenger with someone who worked on the campaign. They told him I was fine.

Soon the rumors and reports were out of control. The United Nations was going to be attacked next, and our daughter, Cita, was handling payroll for the campaign at another office not far from there, at Fortieth and Lexington. The towers collapsed, and from our windows, we could see the droves of people walking north, covered in white dust.

The scenes were unforgettable. The election was halted.

I called Cita, who was with my sister, Yamilla. I told her to leave and drive home. I grabbed my bag and ran downstairs.

"We'll meet at home," I promised her.

I hugged Michael, who had been with me since before sunrise, and he began walking home to Brooklyn.

I started driving north. Nobody was getting into Manhattan, and everybody was heading out. The streets were rivers of people. All I could see were the red taillights ahead of me, all those cars trying to find a way out of the city. Soon I started picking up strangers to help them out.

When we finally got home, I knew we could have won that day. Our path to victory was real. On top of all the horrors of the day, the fucking terrorists robbed New York of our first Puerto Rican mayor. We had been polling every day and were carrying 70 percent of the Black vote and 90 percent of the Latino vote. We knew we could get the 20 percent of the white vote that we needed.

My family was all safe, thank God. But the chaos was only just beginning.

Voting restarted two weeks later, on September 25, with no votes from September 11 being counted. New York, and the world, had changed profoundly. We ended up in first place with 36 percent of the vote, four points shy of full victory, and headed into a runoff against Green two weeks later.

What followed was stunning. Rudy Giuliani started suggesting that he should stick around as mayor beyond the end of his term. That would involve a change to the city's constitution so he could hold on to power. For reasons that are hard to fathom, Mark Green said this was a good idea. He was a Democrat supporting a Republican holding on to power beyond the law. He was also desperate to buy into the idea that Giuliani, as unpopular as he had been, had become some kind of protector of the city against terrorists.

We said no right away. I had a good relationship with Green's campaign manager and called him up in dismay. "Are you insane? The constitution of the United States was not suspended after the civil war started," I said. "The transfer of power must continue. Hopefully you'll get another candidate who can face the new reality and new challenges without trying to change the constitution."

Freddy and I met with Giuliani in person to say the same. Of course, I had worked with him and knew him well. But that didn't change our message. "I know you're coming from a good place and things are very unsettling in the city," I told him. "But we need to be able to follow the transfer of power. That's how you measure the strength of a democracy."

Giuliani's fever dream did not become reality. It would have needed legislative approval, and there was no desire in the state assembly to do so. But the unthinkable and the unspeakable were now acceptable in politics and the media, and our runoff election was just two weeks away.

Green shifted his campaign to an unsubtly racist question: are we ready for a Puerto Rican mayor when the city is going through the most traumatic political and economic experience in living memory? They appealed to white voters by claiming that Ferrer was borderline irresponsible, dividing the city and supporting higher taxes at a time when the city could not afford to change direction. All of a sudden, our alliance with Al Sharpton played into the worst racist attitudes you could imagine. The *New York Post* published a racist cartoon of Freddy kissing Sharpton's ass, which was typical of the right-wing trash peddled by that tabloid. What was less typical was the way in which one of Green's operatives reprinted the cartoon as a flyer and sent it to white voters across the city. Now we had a Democratic candidate asking voters, "Do you want Al Sharpton to become your next police commissioner?"

That kind of attitude seeped into coverage of the whole campaign. The *New York Times Magazine* featured both candidates. Mark Green was dressed in a suit; Freddy was in a guayabera shirt. Green's supporters showed up to one of our rallies and started throwing cheap chancleta sandals with a photo of Freddy at us. It was not pretty. I keep one of those chancletas on my desk as a constant reminder of who I am and what I stand for—a proud Latino always ready to kick ass for my community.

I must have slept two or three hours a night every day for those two weeks before the runoff. We opened an account with a hotel in Soho that was owned by a donor to Freddy's campaign. I would finish work at 3:00 a.m. and be back at work at 5:30.

As if that were not enough, we had welcomed Miguel into our family earlier that year. Luz brought the baby to the office so I could see him briefly in the middle of our madness.

We lost the runoff by all of 16,000 votes out of more than 800,000 cast across the city.

The white voters did not turn out for our candidate; they voted for Green. Our strategy of a Black and Brown coalition had worked before 9/11, but the city had changed in a matter of days. The thinly veiled prejudice of Green's campaign had succeeded. It felt like a textbook case of political racism directed toward a whole group of people who were being told they should never be in charge of the city of New York. Freddy was an aspirational candidate for Latinos and Blacks, with a solid coalition behind him. He came from the Bronx, where he had been borough president for years. The Bronx was our aspirational place. But it was not an aspirational place for white voters, who wanted to move to Manhattan or Brooklyn.

If Freddy had won, things would have become complicated. I was the only guy in the room who had spent time running city agencies. So everyone was clear, as the election approached, that I should be the chief of staff and do that job for a couple of years. Instead, I was the one assigned to continue to work with the Green campaign in the general election. Green now faced Mike Bloomberg, who was nominally the Republican candidate.

I helped organize a meeting at our campaign headquarters between Green and the Black and Latino leaders who had supported Freddy. People were peppering Green with questions. They were angry about the ads, about the flyer featuring the *Post* cartoon, about the whole tone of his campaign.

"Listen," Green told them, "I don't need you to win. But I need you to govern."

The room went crazy. People were screaming at him and walking out.

"Then call us when you win," said my old friend, and now member of Congress Nydia Velázquez as the room emptied.

The bitterness was everywhere. My partner, Roberto, told me he was unsure about supporting Green. "If you decide to go along with Green, that's fine," I said. "But then you're like everybody else." Roberto decided not to support Green, choosing instead to blast him in the media.

When the Green team approached me to join them in government if they won, my answer was simple. "I'm not doing that," I told them. "Your guy is an asshole. I already worked for an asshole. His name is Rudy Giuliani."

One asshole was more than enough for one career.

Still, I wanted the Democratic candidate to win. So I was part of the prep team, alongside the great African American strategist Bill Lynch, as Green readied to debate Bloomberg. The prep did not go well. Without warning, Lynch and the other Freddy people walked out, and I was the only one left behind. Then Green walked out, and his campaign manager stayed behind. "I will tell you," I said, "it will take an enormous amount of discipline for me to vote for Mark Green." Green bombed the debate. He came across as I expected, as a pompous and arrogant rich boy. That was hard to do when he was running against Bloomberg—one of the richest people in New York City.

When election day came around, Roberto shut down the Bronx Democratic Party headquarters. There was no political activity in the borough that day. No operation to turn out the vote in the borough where Freddy was from. If people wanted to campaign, they could. But nothing was organized by the party, and I stayed home.

Green went on to lose to Bloomberg in the general election by 2 percentage points, and I wasn't upset. Bloomberg won with half the Latino vote. He wasn't even a Republican, but he fit the bill. Green had bought into the notion that the city needed a powerful white man to lead it. It had started with Giuliani and his autocratic white view of the world. And it had come back to bite Green because he wasn't as much of a powerful white man as his billionaire opponent with a history of philanthropic work.

———

FREDDY RAN AGAIN IN 2005 AGAINST MAYOR BLOOMBERG. IT WAS a David and Goliath contest, even though we were in a better position as an organization, with a very professional campaign manager. But winning was a long shot. It was one of those things that happens only in telenovelas, where the poor domestic help marries the son of the rich family: an unlikely dream.

Bloomberg wasn't just the incumbent; he had more money than God.

His campaign spent it, in part, on trashing our candidate. We hated 3:00 p.m. because that was the time of day when they would dump all of their negative research on Freddy. Every reporter would call us with some new negative story. Little things that Freddy had done as borough president during his many, many years in office. For instance, people would go to him and say their kid was in jail, but he was a really good kid. So Freddy would send someone to interview the parent and find out how good the kid was. Then he would send a letter to the parole board saying the kid was from a good family, with roots in the community, asking for him to come out on parole.

Every day at 3:00 p.m., it was like it was raining on us. They had so many resources. You try to do your own negative research on your own candidate. But we did not have the money to research every letter and every little thing that someone had done in two decades of elected office. They did. So we never knew what the fuck was going to hit us. It was never a huge story, but it was like dying from a thousand little cuts. Every day we were bleeding.

We were depending on the Latino community, but there was less enthusiasm this time around. Bloomberg was autocratic, but he wasn't a bad mayor. He was as much a Republican as I was a Baltimore Orioles fan. He supported Republicans financially, but he hadn't really played an active role in the party before he was elected. He was a Republican mayor, but he managed the city as a technocrat, which at the end of the day is all that anybody wants. They just want the trains to run, the garbage to be picked up, and all the other things that add up to the quality of life in a city.

The only narrative we had was the reality of the city today— that there are two New Yorks. There is the Michael Bloomberg New York, and then there is the New York for most of us who live in the neighborhoods. It would work well for Bill de Blasio a few years later. But when you have a good narrative, you need the resources for it to catch fire the way it needs to. We just didn't have those resources, while Bloomberg did.

Freddy always enthusiastically believed that he was going to win. I admire it when people maintain an enthusiasm that isn't grounded in reality. You need to have that if you're going to get up every morning and talk to voters at a subway stop at 7:00 a.m., ahead of ten events during the day, before you arrive home exhausted at the end of it all.

We won the Democratic primary but lost the election by almost 20 points.

I worked on one more campaign against Bloomberg, four years later, serving as a consultant to Billy Thompson. Billy was the first African American candidate in the general election since David Dinkins, which was already a long time ago. He was a lot like Freddy: a good guy who had great ideas, with a decent record in office—in his case, as the city's comptroller. He was a great counterpart to Bloomberg, whose persona is built around knowing how to run big companies. Bill had run the finances of a big city, and the pension fund was doing well after he had diversified it. We had created a Black-Latino alliance that had voted for Freddy twice. It was easy to explain to Latinos that African Americans had voted with us twice; now it was time to vote for their viable candidate.

Besides, Bloomberg had already served eight years and was changing the city's charter to allow him to run for a third term. People don't mind it if you are rich and doing a decent job of running the city. But they dislike it when you are changing the rules of the game to win. It felt much like Giuliani trying to stay on as mayor after the 9/11 attacks. The city council rolled over because they also wanted another term. Sometimes when people are elected, they drink their own Kool-Aid and believe they are the only ones who can do what they have done. They forget that there's life at the end of being an elected official or that there's an entire universe of good people doing good things who are ready to take their place.

However, Bloomberg once again had something we did not: $108 million to spend on his campaign. We had $9 million. Naturally, we lost, but this time by only a few points.

We ended up as the heroes after each losing campaign in New York. We always fought the good fight of an underfunded, smart minority candidate. We were always close to power but never got our hands on it because the system is created in such a way that the odds are overwhelming.

Over time, the Latino coalition matured in the city. Black and Latino voters were sharing neighborhoods, realizing that our fates were bound together. Our streets were beginning to change, becoming gentrified as housing became increasingly unaffordable for the working class. We learned that we needed to vote together for candidates who would try to stop that. That maturing coalition paved the way for Bill de Blasio and Eric Adams as the next two mayors of New York. It paved the way for de Blasio to create universal preschool education, a transformational initiative. All the research shows that middle-class children do better because their education begins before they start school. To allow young children to learn what their affluent counterparts learn—that changes lives.

Unity comes not from some imagined narrative or a projected identity but from shared experience and shared values. To build a coalition, across Latino communities and across different groups, we must identify what we share and how we can progress together.

CHAPTER 7

The Senators

I HAVE ALWAYS BEEN DRIVEN BY DATA. I LOVE NUMBERS AND what they can tell you. In looking at elections in New York, out of all the knowledge that exists in the city, I have spent a lot of time looking at statistics on subway usage. I look at voting patterns at big polling sites. I want to know where to deploy, where to concentrate resources. Nowadays, so much information is just a Google search away. But when I started my campaign career, it was all on paper and in my head.

That is how I knew back in 1998 that an upstart candidate for the US Senate seat for New York stood no chance of getting the Democratic nomination.

My partner, Roberto, thought it would be a good first campaign for me to help this long-running congressman from Brooklyn.

"Can I get some data?" I asked. The data were not encouraging. He was in single digits, running against Mark Green, the city's well-known public advocate, and Geraldine Ferraro, the first woman to be a vice-presidential candidate for a major party in this country's history. He was running against a fierce city fixture and the queen of Democratic politics.

"Why do you want me to lose? This is my first paid campaign," I told Roberto. "This guy is going to lose."

"You only look at the science part of campaigns," he replied. "Campaigns are science and magic. I'm telling you, this guy is going to win."

The three of us met at the Bronx Democratic Party offices: Roberto and I and this enthusiastic, motormouth candidate. He wouldn't stop talking about how he was going to win. He would win the Jewish votes. He would get the Latino votes because we were going to deliver them for him. He was from Brooklyn, which represented the biggest chunk of votes.

His name was Chuck Schumer, and he convinced me. He was a big character and knowledgeable about everything. I thought that if he talked like this to voters, people would vote for him. He also had policy solutions for everyone. He was in favor of the US Navy leaving Vieques and had said so publicly before meeting us. For us, that was a litmus test. He promised that his first trip would be to Puerto Rico. And he promised that his first judicial recommendation would be a Puerto Rican jurist. He ultimately delivered on all those promises.

He reminded me of Ed Koch, although he was less abrasive and more careful with his pronouncements. Schumer would not talk about things when he knew nothing about them, unlike Koch. But they shared a can-do persona, and I loved them both for it.

His numbers were less charming, and his path to success was a very steep climb. He needed the support of every community leader, and he worked hard to win them over. He wanted the support of the Dominican community, and Roberto convinced the elected officials in the Bronx to back him. I put together a meeting with Linares and other leaders in Washington Heights. Everyone agreed to support him, including Congresswoman Nydia Velázquez. While Schumer was working the neighborhoods to build support, Ferraro rested on her enormous name recognition. We were in the streets all the time, and we never saw her or her campaign. As for Mark Green, every time he met a voter, he lost a vote. Schumer's campaign was well funded, and his real challenge came from the contrast—a woman candidate, not someone with a similar profile. There are more women voters than men voters, and the Ferraro campaign didn't need to spend anything to tell people who she was. We thought she was a shoo-in.

We concentrated on radio and mail and on driving up the Latino vote. It was the first time that Latino voters had been targeted with a mail campaign in this kind of election, and it worked. Our media outreach was run by Mark Guma and Josh Isay, and they worked wonders. Schumer won the primary by 24 points over Ferraro and 31 points over Green.

The general election was also a tough proposition. The incumbent Republican senator, Al D'Amato, was everywhere. Whenever we went to talk to a community leader, we would find that D'Amato had already met them or was about to meet with them. We were playing catch-up with someone who was seeking his fourth term as a senator. Our strength—apart from the fact that the state was far less conservative than it had been when D'Amato was first elected—was Schumer himself. He was this big persona that D'Amato just wasn't. D'Amato was great over a coffee but less so discussing the future of our community. There wasn't a meeting we had that we didn't leave with a full endorsement for our candidate.

Schumer himself was never shy about meeting with anyone. His work ethic amazes me, even though I have been doing this job for so long. He is a fantastic performer who never tires.

In that sense, we have a lot in common. Like him, I will go to any meeting with anyone, anywhere, if it helps build our coalition. I spent eight years building the Hispanic Federation, creating something from nothing. It was as if I walked around with four mirrors pretending that there were four of me, rather than just one, because I met with everybody. Before that, working for Ed Koch, I went to the tiniest places to talk about citizenship. It never scared me. I didn't care where I went, even in the 1980s, when crime was still high. Maybe I should have been more careful, but that wasn't me. If someone told me there were going to be fifty people without papers in some basement, I would show up to that basement.

For Schumer, that unstoppable spirit translated into Latino votes across the city. Republicans never paid a lot of attention to Latinos anyway. But those votes helped push Schumer to a stunning victory, unseating D'Amato by a margin of 10 points.

———

MY PROFILE IN POLITICS CHANGED AFTER THE SCHUMER VICTORY. Little more than a year later, the second US Senate seat for New York opened up for an even better known candidate: Hillary Rodham Clinton. As first lady, emerging from the trauma of her husband's impeachment, she was both high profile and untested as a candidate herself. She began her campaign with a listening tour, and I was asked to help her listen to the Latino community across the state.

I didn't know what to expect from her, but I was blown away. I had never met someone of her caliber: someone who could enter a room of people she had never met before and engage with them as if she already knew them. These were curated groups, to be sure. They were not random meetings. When we went to Monroe College in the Bronx, we knew how many attendees were students, how many were neighbors, how many were community leaders and elected officials. We would brief her, of course. But after one briefing, she had ingested everything. Her command of the facts is stunning.

The biggest Latino event in those days was the Somos New York legislative conference in Albany, uniting the Latino community across the state. Clinton was speaking at a plenary session event that we had created for her, and we were planning the most important things she needed to say. Some of her advisers wanted to write a speech for her, but she insisted on speaking just from bullet points. She proceeded to deliver a speech that was flawless and seamless. She wove one bullet into the next and added some more of her own. Afterward she signed copies of her best-selling book, *It Takes a Village*. She mingled with them all and then went to a smaller VIP area, where she met with a group of people we had briefed her about. She stayed to talk to these people as if they were her long-lost friends. She was a superstar, and the community loved her for it. Any place we traveled with her, we needed security to manage the crowds. It was pandemonium. She never lost her cool. She was unfazed by it all.

There was no bigger issue for the Puerto Rican community than the issue of Vieques, which posed an even greater challenge for Hillary than for other Democrats. Her husband was still the commander-in-chief as she ran for the Senate, and she was extremely cautious about being seen to influence his foreign policy. She had suffered, after all, from the searing experience of leading the efforts to reform health care early in his presidency. So her initial position on the US Navy's presence in Vieques was "That's an area that I want to stay away from."

"Well, you can't," I told her, "because it's what we talk about the most in the Puerto Rican community and the number one issue for our leaders. Keep in mind that we are the largest share of the Latino vote."

She quickly realized that she needed to take a position, which was the right one: the navy needed to leave Vieques. Because of national security, we needed another place to continue to train, but it couldn't be Vieques. I don't know what she did behind closed doors, but that position soon became the official policy of the United States. Her listening tour began in July; by December, President Clinton had announced an end to live-fire training in Vieques and a full end to exercises within five years.

By the time the real campaign came around in 2000, we were tasked with the fieldwork in all the Latino communities across the state. That took me to Latino pockets upstate in Buffalo, Syracuse, and Rochester. Of course, the bulk of the votes was in New York City. But the campaign had resources, so I asked for support and got it. It was like living with a rich family. By the time we were processing payroll for all the get-out-the-vote workers on election day, it was several hundred people. We had field coordinators everywhere. I spent my day running from place to place, jumping between the top Latino voting locations across the city all day long.

We won comfortably against Republican Rick Lazio by a margin of 12 points. If Giuliani hadn't melted down after just a few weeks of campaigning, with a highly turbulent affair and divorce, perhaps it would have been closer. But that was Rudy Giuliani. He would have lost to Hillary anyway.

The month after winning her race, she invited us to the White House Christmas party. It was the first time I had walked into the president's home, the seat of American power. We arrived a little early and got a tour of the executive mansion. I had never seen so many Christmas trees in one place. Every tree meant something. This kind of thing always baffles me. In my head, it's just a tree with red ribbons or green ribbons. But there was significance in all of it, and every tree was special. Luz, on the other hand, appreciates all of that.

"It's just a Christmas tree," I told her.

"It's a Christmas tree in the White House," she replied.

Regardless of our opposing sentiments about the tree, we were amazed we were there. We took pictures in front of Nancy Reagan's portrait and then Jackie Kennedy's. We met Hillary and Bill Clinton in the receiving line, and we talked about New York, including Bill Clinton's account of his visit to the Bronx for his wife's campaign.

It was a strange time to be partying in the White House because the world was still waiting to learn who would succeed President Clinton in office. The presidential recount between Al Gore and George W. Bush was ongoing through the holiday party season and would not be resolved until mid-December. We thought President Bush needed to be defeated. His emphasis on the military and tax cuts was never my cup of tea. Al Gore ran on a platform of economic reform and government involvement in fixing the climate catastrophe and helping poor people, of whom Latinos are a large share. In retrospect, Bush seems un nene de teta in comparison to the next generation of Republicans led by twice-impeached Donald Trump. But let's not be romantic—Bush was a bad president for this country.

———

BY THE TIME HILLARY WAS RUNNING FOR PRESIDENT HERSELF, IN 2007, our children were old enough and mature enough to make informed political decisions for themselves. We would have discussions about the election, and we adored both Obama and Clinton. But our children would say that while they loved Hillary, we needed to move to the next generation of leaders. As a New York political consultant, I didn't have a mechanism to become involved in a national campaign. It made sense to continue to be involved in significant local elections. I wanted Hillary to win the nomination because we would have elected our first woman president. But I wasn't upset with the outcome. Instead, we got our first Black president. This was a win-win in my view.

From my perspective, and based on the Latino community's priorities, as much as we loved President Obama, we were sometimes frustrated that things didn't move quickly enough. At points, I would remind myself that we had felt the same during the Koch years, when we controlled everything and still couldn't move quickly enough. I felt that Obama's main unfinished business was to move the needle on immigration. His DACA program for so-called Dreamers—the undocumented Americans who had arrived here as children—was the bare minimum. I could see it in my own household. If either Luz or I had been born on the other side of Eagle Pass, Texas—in Piedras Negras—and our family had crossed the border when we were two years old, are you telling me that we are not American? That we have another fucking country to go to? If we hadn't been born in Puerto Rico, we would have been Dreamers. We would have had to apply every couple of years for something that should have been a right.

The Democrats had control of the whole of Congress, but they were not moving the needle. We had too many marginal Democrats who depended on being silent on immigration because the issue has been demonized and weaponized against the party. So even when we controlled everything, we did nothing. I was at one congressional Hispanic caucus dinner where Obama was talking, and a whole bunch of young people interrupted his speech to start screaming at him. For a second, I agreed with them. You know what? Yeah. You should recognize this failure on your watch. Then I reminded myself that it wasn't him: it wasn't high enough on the agenda because Republicans and too many marginal Democrats would never vote in favor of immigration reform with a path to citizenship.

All the data suggest that we need immigrants in this country. There are jobs that go unfilled when immigration is stopped. The immigrants who are here belong here. Their children do better. They go to college and get the next job. My brother-in-law owns farms in southern New Jersey. We don't talk about politics, but what he says makes me believe that he's Republican. One day he told me how mad he was at Republicans because he normally employed Mexicans and Central Americans to work on his farm. I know enough about him to know that he's a decent boss, that he doesn't exploit people, that he pays well and has good accommodations for his workers. But he couldn't hire people because of the attacks on immigration. The Republican Party has changed fundamentally. I saw what Ronald Reagan did in 1986. Now the Republican Party's anti-immigrant narrative has paralyzed our ability to tackle this issue, and now with the surge of asylum seekers, even Democrats like Mayor Eric Adams are adding wood to the fire. I have no idea how we can go back to something more acceptable, or even what that something is. Someone needs lots of political courage, and I see no one out there who fits the bill.

———

KIRSTEN GILLIBRAND WAS A MEMBER OF THE HOUSE REPRESENTing an upstate district when Hillary Clinton quit her Senate seat to become secretary of state in 2009 under President Obama. We all thought that Caroline Kennedy would become the next senator for New York, taking the seat her uncle Bobby had once held. But the day before the announcement, my partner, Roberto, who was close to then Governor David Paterson, told me that Kennedy wasn't going to make it. We were both pushing for Freddy Ferrer to take the job, but it was hard to read what Paterson was thinking.

The next day, I was on the USS *Intrepid*, hosting a birthday party for Miguel, when I saw that Roberto was trying to call me. I ignored him a couple of times before Luz tapped me on the shoulder. "Roberto called me," she said. "It's important that you call him."

I stepped out of the party and called him back. He wanted to know if I knew Gillibrand because she was going to be the next senator for New York. I said yes. "I read somewhere that she sleeps with a rifle under her bed," I joked. "And she voted against an immigration bill."

Roberto told me the more urgent news: she wanted to meet us. That day. In a few hours. By this point, my voice mail included calls from Governor Paterson, from the new senator, and from our friends and partners at Global Strategy, the consultants who had done the polling in Gillibrand's House race.

"Why do we want this in our lives?" I asked Roberto.

"I'm asking you," he said. "Please be at this meeting."

I had little choice but to show up at our offices on Broadway to meet a woman who was already being demonized for her votes on immigration and gun control.

That wasn't who showed up at our office that cold January afternoon in 2009. She was warm, inquisitive, and direct, explaining that she had this big thing she was now doing, that she needed our help and was willing to learn and willing to change. I asked her about the rifle, partly joking, but also because I had expected her to show up with it. Why just leave it under your bed?

"Luis," she said, "I'm from upstate. Hunting is a part of life up there. It doesn't mean that I own a semiautomatic rifle. Having it under the bed is a bit of hyperbole. I was trying to get elected to Congress in a red district."

"You voted against an immigration bill," I shot back.

"Luis, that was a reconciliation bill that had seven thousand things attached to it," she explained. "At the time, it didn't feel like I had voted against an immigration bill."

I knew from my own time in government that if you cannot pass something on its own, you attach it to something that needs to pass. Sometimes people make those tough choices.

"You've got to help me," she said.

What I saw was someone who had a real desire to learn what our community was all about. What I saw was someone who was asking us to try to understand her position.

"It's up to Luis," said Roberto.

I hate it when Roberto does that. He does it whenever he wants to do something but I'm on the other side opposing it. It's up to Luis. We have known each other for so long that we know when to play that card. And we play it very few times. I have invoked it too, so I know what it sounds like.

"I really want to think about this," I told them. "Thanks for coming to meet us."

The following day, in the Latino media, the headlines weren't pretty. Gillibrand was the devil with two heads. Everybody had been expecting Kennedy, this iconic liberal New Yorker, the daughter of the beloved president. We had all grown up with a photo of JFK hanging on the wall next to a picture of a very white Jesus Christ. She was the daughter of one of the angels in our homes. I knew this kind of reaction was unjust, and I had just talked to Gillibrand. I knew that she didn't have two heads. I understood her tough political choices because she had needed to be elected in a red district. Other than a handful of issues, she and I agreed on almost everything.

So I called Roberto and said, "We're going to help her."

We didn't have much time to change her profile in the community. There was just a year and a half before the Democratic primaries, when she would have to campaign for the Senate seat she had just been handed. All we could do was use our human capital: use our relationships to get in the door and ask people to give her a chance.

That same day, I set up a lunch between Gillibrand and Rossana Rosado, the then publisher of *El Diario*, which was a consequential voice in the Latino community. I asked my successor at the Hispanic Federation to meet with her too. Then we called all the Latino elected officials to meet her.

All these meetings were horrific gambles for her because the only way people were willing to meet was if the conversations were on the record. Within days of her appointment, she was in the hot seat, being grilled by Latino community leaders about her real feelings. She courageously agreed to the meetings. This was her listening tour, taking place after her appointment.

Gillibrand studied like there was no tomorrow. Like she was cramming for the orals for a dissertation. But it wasn't just a high school or college test. She evolved on immigration and became one of the best allies we have in the Senate.

As a result of her relentless hard work, Latinos really showed up for her. She won her primary with 76 percent of the vote, and she won the general election by a margin of 28 points—in the 2010 cycle that was a catastrophe for Democrats across the country.

———

THE YEAR HILLARY CLINTON RAN FOR PRESIDENT AGAIN WAS A very busy one for me. It was the year of the ascendancy of *Hamilton*. A lot of my waking hours were dedicated to trying to understand this phenomenon. Lin-Manuel needed some structure, as his fame and his musical were exploding. We'd had a taste of it from the experience of *In the Heights*. However, *Hamilton* was something entirely different. All of a sudden, Lin-Manuel was a superstar, and I had to protect my kid. It's the most important job I have; I have always been clear about that. Politics is always second. Too much was happening in his life for me to do anything else. I was spending my time with my daughter setting up financial support around him, getting to know the people involved in his life, being available to discuss what he might want to do next.

When election day 2016 came around, we voted in the morning and then Lin-Manuel and I flew to Mexico City to promote his movie *Moana*. Like the rest of the country and the world, we were certain that Hillary was winning. We watched the results come in together, even though Lin-Manuel says he hates politics. He spent the entire night FaceTiming with his college friends as they all watched TV and freaked out about what was happening. When I freak out, I prefer to do it alone. In public, I need to maintain my composure and be the voice of reason. I'm not allowed to freak out. I don't know enough about the electoral college to predict everything, but I knew enough about elections to realize that Hillary was going to lose. I told Lin-Manuel to go to sleep because it was over.

We were no different from the rest of New York in our assumptions about Donald Trump. We knew he was an asshole who said stupid things. We all figured he would continue to be an asshole who would continue to say stupid things. We had no idea he would become an ideological dark force. He would say bad things on the campaign trail, but he also fired people on TV who were really not fired. It all seemed like a show. He would blatantly lie about where Obama had been born just to get attention for himself. Part of me continued to believe that all his hysterics were just histrionics, not that he would ultimately lead a movement to bring the most extreme and nativist forces of this country together under one banner. Not in my wildest dreams, or nightmares, did I envision that his movement would threaten democracy as we know it.

Trump's first year in office changed my views. Throughout that year, I could see how people such as Steve Bannon were realigning themselves. By 2017, I knew that we had to work harder than we had ever worked before to get this guy out of office and begin to recruit the next generation of leaders. That was when Latino Victory came to me with the opportunity to become chair of their board. I saw that as a vehicle to do what I have always done: to organize Latinos, only this time on a national scale.

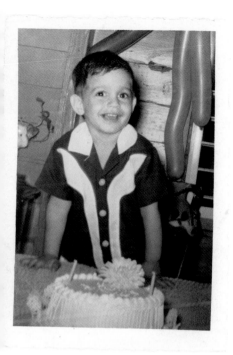

Turning two years old in Vega Alta, Puerto Rico, at my grandparents' house. *Photo courtesy of the Miranda Family*

At Playa Cerro Gordo with my mother, Eva, and my dad, Güisin, in the summer of 1958. *Photo courtesy of the Miranda Family*

Performing a monologue at a high school show in Vega Alta's town square, May 1971. *Photo courtesy of the Miranda Family*

With my great aunt, Mamá Suncha, at my first wedding in 1973. *Photo courtesy of the Miranda Family*

My friend Nydia Velázquez and I celebrating our arrival to New York and the beginning of our graduate studies at New York University. *Photo courtesy of the Miranda Family*

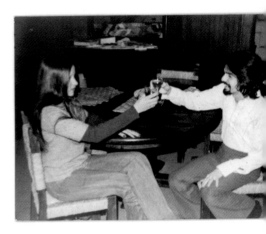

Strolling through Washington Square Park in winter 1976. *Photo courtesy of the Miranda Family*

My wedding to Luz in Somerset, New Jersey, on September 16, 1978. *Photo courtesy of the Miranda Family*

Our first summer as a family in 1980 at NYU housing on Bleeker Street. *Photo courtesy of the Miranda Family*

Lin-Manuel speaks at my swearing-in ceremony in 1987. *Wagner/LaGuardia Archives*

Mayor Ed Koch and the Latinos in his administration in 1987 on the steps of City Hall. *Wagner/LaGuardia Archives*

Walking from St. Patrick's Cathedral to our reception after our Catholic wedding on March 27, 1993. *Photo courtesy of the Miranda Family*

The 1993 Hispanic Federation press conference with then assemblyman Rober Ramírez (*seated center*), who would lat become MirRam's cofounder, and t three Latino leaders who would lat become presidents of the Hispanic Federation: Frankie Miranda (*seated lef* Lorraine Cortés-Vázquez, and Lilli Rodriguez Lopez (*seated right respe tively*). *Photo courtesy of the Hispan Federation*

Then House Representative Chuck Schumer participating in the 1994 Hispanic Federation press conference, announcing the release of the "Hispanic New Yorkers on Nueva York" survey. *Photo courtesy of the Hispanic Federation*

Talking to the press on Freddy Ferrer's primary day in 2001. *Photo courtesy of Freddy Ferrer*

Celebrating Father's Day in 2014 on our stoop in Inwood. *Photo courtesy of the Miranda Family*

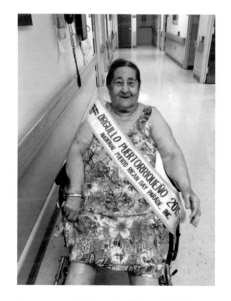

Our nanny, Edmunda "Mundi" Claudio, at the Isabella Geriatric Center, celebrates the 2015 Puerto Rican Day Parade. *Photo courtesy of the Miranda Family*

Serving food to victims of Hurricane Maria in Vega Alta, Puerto Rico, in 2017. *Photo courtesy of the Hispanic Federation*

Fighting for federal aid t Puerto Rico in Washing ton, DC, after Hurrican Irma and Maria devastate Puerto Rico in 2017. *Pho courtesy of the Hispan Federation*

Introducing Letitia James to an audience of seniors on Election Day in 2018. *Photo Courtesy of HBO and Siempre, Luis*

Celebrating the opening of *Hamilton* in Puerto Rico at San Juan's Centro de Bellas Artes, which raised $15 million for the arts in Puerto Rico, 2019. *Photo by Emilio Madrid-Kuser*

n-Manuel and Cita with Miguel at his 2019 high hool graduation from York Prep. *Photo courtesy the Miranda Family*

Lin-Manuel, Hillary Clinton, and I in 2021 at the *In the Heights* community screening event. *Photo by Emmanuel Abreu*

Lin-Manuel, Luz, and I cutting the ribbon at the Galería Lin-Manuel Miranda in 2022 for an exhibit highlighting our family's work in Puerto Rico after Hurricane Maria. *Photo courtesy of the Miranda Family*

Visiting coffee growers in Puerto Rico in 2022 as part of the Hispanic Federation's coffee initiative. *Photo courtesy of the Hispanic Federation*

Welcoming migrants to New York City in 2023 at the Port Authority of New York and New Jersey. *Photo courtesy of the Hispanic Federation*

Senator Kirsten Gillibrand and I speak about her upcoming 2024 reelection campaign. *Photo courtesy of the Miranda Family*

Trump became a bit of an obsession for me. You can ask my family members. I was on social media all day long. Now I had some resources that we had not had before, thanks to *Hamilton*. So I could personally donate to candidates in ways that I couldn't before. I also gave money to independent expenditure groups that were totally anti-Trump.

Latino Victory, however, was the real vehicle for me to marry my passions for electing new candidates and bringing together different communities. The organization was founded in 2014 by the actor and producer Eva Longoria and the former DNC finance chair Henry Muñoz to drive Latino voters and elect more Latino officials across the country. I was clear from the beginning that Latinidad, our shared identity, wasn't the only measure of success. There were real ideological boundaries that I wasn't willing to cross. I wouldn't support people whose political elasticity moved them to places where I could not go. Especially when it came to immigration and the border. I understand that we cannot open our borders. But I do know that when we open ourselves to new immigrants, we continue to attract the best people from their countries of origin. We have nothing to fear. Immigrants work disproportionately for the good of society in general to build a community that can help them advance. So immigration became tied together with the need for an economy that really takes care of people. Government has to play an enormous role in people's lives because it's the only organization with the shared resources to change lives.

That was very clear when Hurricane Maria hit Puerto Rico. We could each do our best, but the federal government was the only entity with the resources to help in a large way. Instead, Trump stuck it to Puerto Rico in the worst possible way. My life revolved around Puerto Rico, getting rid of Trump, and electing Latinos through Latino Victory.

When the chance came around to fire Trump in 2020, my mind was very clear. I knew that Bernie Sanders was the choice of most of the staff at Latino Victory, and I believed he could not win. But I was in a position where I couldn't make independent decisions. I was chair of a board and needed to bring everyone along.

On top of that, I was close to Kirsten Gillibrand, who was also running for president. One day, she called me to say she was heading upstate and would it be OK to stop by our house. She showed up with security, three staff members, and two kids. It was great spending time with her, but I couldn't support her.

It took a little while for the board of Latino Victory to unanimously support Biden. But we did. Just before the Arizona primary, we organized a local event to support Biden. Our staff was apprehensive. Almost all the national Latino organizations were either supporting Bernie Sanders or waiting on the sidelines.

We got so much grief for not supporting Bernie Sanders. However, I just knew that he couldn't win. For me, defeating Trump with someone decent was more important than losing with someone closer to my political beliefs and having Trump for four more years. But not everyone agreed with me. I had been working on Latino issues for a long time. I had never heard of Bernie Sanders being a defender of our rights. Perhaps he didn't have the platform that he has now. Our eclectic Latino political community, I strongly believed, needed someone who was good enough on the issues but who would come across—and have a history—as a moderate.

I had met Joe Biden several times. We had often seen him with the Obamas at events at the White House. He always came across as a good guy who would take care of business, who knew what government can and should do. And that was exactly what we got. I wasn't looking for a Bernie Sanders or his ideology. I was looking to get rid of someone who I believe is dangerous to the overwhelming majority of people in this country. Certainly to Jews, certainly to African Americans, certainly to Latinos, certainly to queer people, and certainly to women. Trump is dangerous to democracy itself.

I see these people at Trump's rallies. I am sure many are good people who love their families and go to church. But they're sharing space with neo-Nazis and racists. They are just totally lost. They are ideologically at sea. That's what a daily quota of *Fox News* is capable of doing.

Many of my progressive friends thought Bernie was the candidate for change in the Democratic Party. They said this was the moment to move our progressive agenda forward. If we lost the White House, we would still be moving our agenda forward.

But I wasn't going to do that. I was stuck in the middle, saying, "Reality is not like this." It was an unusual experience for me. But I trusted my gut, just as my therapist had taught me.

We had to win at all costs, and we did.

CHAPTER 8

A Family Affair

Before Lin-Manuel arrived in our lives, I felt that we were done with children. We had a daughter, and that was enough. Luz had survived cancer, but in getting rid of the cancer, the doctors had damaged her thyroid and parathyroid. She needs to take an obscene amount of vitamin D and calcium to this day. So her pregnancy with Lin-Manuel was high risk, and I was deeply worried. For months, I had a recurring dream of being in front of a coffin, a widower holding hands with two little kids. I never shared those feelings with her, about how I felt during that entire pregnancy, until it was all over. Once Lin-Manuel arrived, I made it very, very clear that I never wanted to experience those feelings again. We had a daughter and now a son. We were done. If we wanted more children, there were plenty of kids out there to adopt.

After reading a poem when I was just thirteen or fourteen years old, I had decided that when I had a son, I would name him Lin-Manuel. The Vietnam War was an enormous cloud hanging over us as I was growing up. People from Puerto Rico enlisted in very large numbers, and they came home damaged or dead. A pamphlet of poems written at the time was called *En Las Manos Del Pueblo* (*In The People's Hands*). One of them was about the poet's son being born while he was a soldier fighting in Vietnam. He named his son Lin-Manuel: Lin, to pay homage to the Vietnamese people he was killing when he had no idea why, and Manuel, to honor his Puerto Rican roots.

When Lin-Manuel was born, there was some pressure to call him Luis, like me and my father. He would have been the third. But I rejected the idea out of hand. *No, this kid is going to be himself. He's not an extension of me.* I remember having these discussions with my family and saying the first step in that individuation process would be to call him something that was important to me but that would be unique to him.

We continued to mix cultures throughout Cita and Lin-Manuel's childhood. I spoke Spanish at home, and so did our nanny, Mundi. But Luz spoke English to the children. So Lin-Manuel spoke Spanish to me and English to his mother. If I ever switched to English, he would correct me. "No, no, no, Daddy," he would say. "Spanish. Spanish." He would do the reverse if Luz switched to Spanish, telling her to speak English. Both Lin-Manuel and Cita spoke English first, and they think in English. But as they were growing up, they spent a month each summer in my hometown, Vega Alta. There was no cable and no internet, and almost no one spoke English. So if they had to defend themselves or ask for something, it had to be in Spanish.

Lin-Manuel has become much better in Spanish because he writes and does so many interviews in Spanish now. But his sister was always the better Spanish speaker.

I was always very close to our daughter, Cita. We are so much alike. She likes the things I like. She doesn't talk about the normal things that bother people. She doesn't talk about hurting people's feelings or having her feelings hurt. That's bullshit. Go handle it and move on. Talk about big things instead.

But when Lin-Manuel was born, we were confronted with sibling rivalry. Cita was six years old, and the school principal asked me one day when the baby was due. "We already have the baby in the house," I explained. It was two weeks after her brother was born, but Cita had not mentioned a thing to anyone at school. She was pretending he didn't exist.

She was never mean about having a new baby in the house. But she clearly behaved like any other older sibling, with an occasional sense of rivalry toward her younger brother. Many years later, she tried to make amends. Just before the first Broadway preview of *In the Heights* in 2008, Cita went into Lin-Manuel's dressing room to apologize for not having been the best sister in the world.

"Cita, this is the first time I'm going to be on a Broadway stage," he said. "I can't do emotional catharsis right now. We can talk about it later."

Cita knew she had a biological dad, who made a few attempts to be part of her life. The Christmas just before Lin-Manuel was born, a present arrived for Cita, and we opened it. It was a shirt that was so big that it fit Luz—who was very pregnant, a few weeks before giving birth. It was from Cita's biological father, but we realized that he didn't care about having a relationship with her. He wanted to have a relationship with Luz.

We never told him that he couldn't have a relationship with Cita, but we agreed that it was really up to him to figure out what he wanted to do. The door would be open if he wanted to walk in. In fact, he came to see her a couple of times when we moved to New York. On Cita's end, she had her chosen dad. Life was good.

With the arrival of Lin-Manuel, I wanted to make sure that no one felt like one child was biologically connected while the other was not. I was always very conscious of that. But I was most concerned about the reaction of my family in Puerto Rico. We hadn't planned to have Lin-Manuel, and I was worried that there had been too little time for the family to be close to Cita. My main concern was my mother. She wore her feelings on her sleeve. She couldn't pretend at all. Cita was a part of the family life, but Lin-Manuel was the first grandchild.

We arrived in Puerto Rico when Lin-Manuel was not even a month old. I need not have worried. Everyone was so cool. Cita continued to be treated just as before, when she was an only child. My brother, Elvin, was a teenager, and Cita spent a lot of time with him and my sister, Yamilla. It felt no different with a new baby who was the first biological grandchild.

My relationship with Cita didn't change. I have always liked to dress nicely and to dress everyone around me. That was a big thing for Cita and me to share. We would go to the stores to buy her birthday dress or her Christmas dress. My wife chooses clothes based on what's practical. I take the opposite approach. I choose things with the recipient in mind, even if I hate it, which is the case with my son. When I buy something for Lin-Manuel, I say, "OK, let's see what I don't like and start there. Let's see what's boring." The absence of patterns is good for Lin-Manuel. He loves anything monochromatic and simple.

Where Lin-Manuel and I bonded was our love of the arts. We went to the movies together. We went to shows together. A lot of what we did together was what I had done with my own father. I wasn't an athletic kid; neither was Lin-Manuel. Everyone except us went to Little League games. Instead, we saw tons of movies together, especially action movies and musicals. We saw every musical out there and every Jean-Claude Van Damme movie ever made. At Hunter Campus Schools, Lin-Manuel's artistic world expanded further with school productions. Of course, he was in every play, and I loved them all. In sixth grade, his school production was four hours of six musicals mashed together. Lin-Manuel remembers all the characters he played. I remember watching a talented kid on stage for four hours. Mercifully my grandchildren perform in productions that are much shorter.

It all started with Lin-Manuel's movies. He was always making his own video movies. Always showing and sharing them. He would watch as much TV as he wanted because we were working, and Mundi watched all the telenovelas she could. Soap operas were his everyday diet. I was no different. For a long time, I couldn't believe how anybody could live without having a telenovela in their life. You need to sit there day after day, watching to learn what happens next. When Mundi was sick and living in a nursing facility toward the end of her life, I would visit every day, or every other day, to watch novelas with her.

Lin-Manuel was in every student production and every chorus he could find. Those were not Cita's interests, even though they both played piano. Regardless of how busy we were, Luz and I always made time to go to the school plays and performances of the local chorus that Lin-Manuel had joined. I too had performed in every student production when I was his age. But Lin-Manuel was different. We knew this was his lane, and he was good at it. He was always inventing and writing. At age nine or ten, he would make his Mother's Day and Father's Day cards with some rhyme he had written. They would come with a mixtape, and each music medley had the spine of Luz's personality or mine. They were not just random songs on a tape. I wanted him to be like Rubén Blades, who graduated with a law degree from Harvard and is one of the greatest artists of all time in Latin America. He and Juan Luis Guerra are my favorite performers because they are storytellers.

"You could be like Rubén Blades," I told Lin-Manuel. "You graduate from one of the greatest schools with a law degree, and then you can do music. If it was good enough for Rubén Blades, why not you?"

I knew that was not going to fly. But you can't blame a dad for trying.

———

OUR CHILDREN TOOK VERY DIFFERENT PATHS AT COLLEGE. CITA was much easier than Lin-Manuel because I agreed with what she wanted. She was good at math and science and less good at the arts, even though she was a good student. I don't know if I convinced her or she convinced herself, but she ended up applying to engineering school. I went to visit all the schools when she applied. We drove her to the Rensselaer Polytechnic Institute in Troy, New York, where she would do her undergraduate work. It was one of the saddest days of my life.

It was the opposite with Lin-Manuel, who drove himself to college. We followed in the car behind because he'd packed so much stuff. Luz was devastated when we left Lin-Manuel; I was devastated when we left Cita. Luz says she likes them equally, but she is much closer emotionally to Lin-Manuel. I have learned to be close to both of them, but for me, it is much easier to work with Cita because we think alike.

We had two stipulations for them. The first was that they couldn't apply to study in New York City. We wanted them to go far enough to be on their own but close enough that we could drive back and forth to visit them in a day. The second was that we would pay for their college. We had seen enough of our friends take on thousands of dollars of debt. We could see how they were struggling to get an apartment and do the stuff that people should be able to do after college. So we worked our asses off. We were always on a ten-month plan, which was like another mortgage that we had to pay every month. Thank God the two of them were not in school at the same time because we wouldn't have been able to afford it. When Cita told us she needed to stay one more semester, Luz burst into tears because it was that much longer that we had to work our asses off to pay this extra mortgage. But we wanted to keep our promise to them, and they both left school without student debt.

Lin-Manuel went to the only school he visited by himself: Wesleyan. I was amazed at how the schools he visited allowed you to select your own curriculum. None of that had been a possibility for me. How different would life have been with an education at one of these amazing colleges? But for our son, there was another compelling reason to love the place: it had a great film department and plenty of student-run theater.

He played the lead in *Jesus Christ Superstar* in his second semester, in a weird avant-garde production where the Romans were Nazis. We rented a bus in New York so we could take all our friends from the neighborhood to the opening. However, we got stuck in a snowstorm, causing a long delay to the start of the show. When we finally arrived, I remember sitting there wondering what was wrong with the original production, while Luz's very Catholic mother was scandalized by the sight of Judas being played by a woman.

In the Heights emerged when Lin-Manuel was just a sophomore at Wesleyan. We took another bus full of friends and family, in typical Miranda fashion. He directed the production and didn't play the lead role of Usnavi. That night, I knew the show was really good, and I knew that he would never go to law school. Our friends from Washington Heights were amazed at how he had recreated our neighborhood on stage.

For his senior project, he wrote another musical that even he would describe as "the one where I made a lot of really great mistakes." I don't even remember what it was. But I knew that he wasn't going to be Rubén Blades. He was going to be like my poor uncle Ernesto, a great actor but pelao, who was always the talk of the family. I was anxious about how he could fulfill his life in the lane he had already chosen.

Not long after he graduated, Lin-Manuel's life choices came into sharp focus. He was living around the corner from us in Upper Manhattan, where he has lived his entire life except for his four years at college. If Broadway was uptown, he would be so much happier. He was a substitute teacher at Hunter, his old high school, and he worked as much as he needed to so that he could pay his rent and cover the basic needs of life. Every Sunday, he and his roommates would come over to our house to watch *The Sopranos* because it was on cable, and they could not afford it. Then Lin-Manuel would raid our refrigerator to take food back to his place. Luz and I enjoyed having them over.

It was at this time that Hunter Campus Schools offered him a full-time position as an English teacher. Lin-Manuel has asked for my advice only a few times in life. I wasn't shy about telling our children that if they were struggling emotionally, they should go to their mom. She is the expert in that department and so much better than me. But if they wanted to get something done, they should come to me. I get stuff done. So Lin-Manuel came to me asking what he should do.

My first thought was to tell him to go talk to his mother. But then I remembered that my parents must have thought I was crazy to leave Puerto Rico for New York. They never said a thing and just helped me to get my ass to New York to do what I thought I needed to do. They did the same when I was about to return to Puerto Rico but instead met Luz, decided to stay in New York, and started my new life with a wife and daughter. My parents never questioned my decisions; they trusted me. So I had no choice but to tell Lin-Manuel, "You can't take that job. You'll never finish *In the Heights*. Your primary responsibility will be to work as a teacher. Finish what you started. Continue as a teaching sub. If it doesn't work out, you're young enough to do whatever the heck you want to do."

I was teaching college myself at his age. I knew how much time it took. There were tests to grade. There were lessons to prepare. It wasn't a job that just lasted from nine to four.

It was seven years between that sophomore's version of *In the Heights* and the musical that opened off Broadway at the 37 Arts Theater. I had never seen anything like that on stage before, and I thought it was going to struggle. I had gone to enough shows to know that the average theatergoer was some white lady from the suburbs who had never heard this kind of music on stage before. She had probably never even heard that music on tape and had never heard of Mega radio. There was enough Spanish for people like me to identify with the characters and the place. On the other hand, there was not enough Spanish to deny entry to English speakers, and you could follow the plot easily enough. This was what worried me as I listened to this creative world that Lin-Manuel had conjured. I loved the representation of Washington Heights as much as I loved *West Side Story*. It was what he knew. We were a struggling middle-class family in a struggling working-class neighborhood. All our friends lived the struggles that are represented on stage. It had not been that long since Luz had cried because Cita needed to stay at school for one more semester.

As good as the show was, the economic reality was more difficult than a great story with great songs. Quite frankly, with no stars, the show would have closed if it hadn't won a Tony award. That was why I did anything and everything the producers asked me to do to help with the show and with that Tony campaign. Unlike an election for public office, you cannot lobby openly for a Tony. But we traveled to Sarasota, Florida, to attend a dinner to talk about our son and *In the Heights* because there were Tony voters there. That included my wife, who couldn't be more uncomfortable with small talk. I could go and sit with a table of strangers and start a conversation with anyone. That isn't the case for Luz, but even she was engaged with people throughout. It was just like a political campaign: we did everything and anything we could to reach people who might or might not end up voting.

I also called on any friends who could help. I reached out to Ken Sunshine, the communications consultant who had been chief of staff to Mayor Dinkins. He represented Barbra Streisand and several other big stars. "Listen, you have to see this show," I told him. "My son has no credits, and you represent Barbra Streisand. But he's good, and he's going places. I want you to be there with him." So Kenny started representing Lin-Manuel pro bono. It was a huge boost to our son and the Tony campaign. I was going to do everything and anything I could for my son not to end up like my talented uncle Ernesto.

On the night of the Tonys, my entire family from Puerto Rico came to New York. Somehow I needed to get fifteen tickets, which wasn't easy. We didn't know the industry very well, but the family wasn't going to miss the big night. We were allocated four tickets—for my immediate family, including Lin-Manuel and Vanessa, his then girlfriend—but we managed to get one more from the show producer. That left us needing another ten. I realized that IBM was one of the main sponsors of the show, and I knew that Stan Litow was part of the IBM Foundation. I had known Stan from the Board of Education and would do anything to get the extra ten tickets.

We were scattered all over the theater, but we got the tickets. Before the show, I told my sister that we needed to be restrained. I made everybody practice how to applaud with more enthusiasm if Lin-Manuel won—but not to scream. Listen, white people don't scream when good things happen. They are very measured in their emotional reactions.

When he won, we all screamed.

That award changed the fortunes of the show, and it changed the course of Lin-Manuel's life. The following day, I was astonished to see Lin-Manuel giving endless interviews in Spanish and English. I took a call from the governor of Puerto Rico, who wanted to congratulate Lin-Manuel because he was holding a Puerto Rican flag during his acceptance speech. That began a division of labor between us. When people asked Lin-Manuel to do things for the worlds of theater or politics, he would tell people to talk to me. "You want to do an event? That's not me," he would say. "Talk to my dad. He'll get it done."

———

MUSIC, THEATER, AND MOVIES WERE INTERWOVEN IN MY FAMILY life. We grew up around music, even without any musicians in our family. For Lin-Manuel's children, it is different. But for me, it grew out of all the singing and dancing that were part of our family's traditions when I was growing up in a half-Catholic family in Puerto Rico. My uncle Ernesto performed in theater in San Juan and had his own Café Teatro, where every weekend there would be poetry and music. At school, I loved performing—acting and singing—even though there was much discussion in the family about how much Ernesto struggled without a steady job. I never saw it as a career option for me, but I still loved performing. As I've proudly mentioned, in my last year of high school, aged sixteen, I won a competition for performing the best monologue in Puerto Rico. It was the voice of a homeless man, telling the story of how he got to that point, taking stock of his life. My father took a Polaroid photo of that moment of me on stage, which I treasure.

Music, however, was more than just a hobby: it was a whole enterprise for me. One day, I came across one of those subscription specials by Columbia Records. You bought the initial twelve records for a dollar and then committed to buying four more for lots of money. The records they offered weren't the usual ones I would have access to. They weren't in Spanish. That was how I bought my first Barbra Streisand record and my first Broadway show LP. I didn't know a lot about these people; I just knew they were in the movies. I still have vinyl albums from that Columbia subscription deal.

Unlike most kids, I didn't need to convince my parents to pay for the records. I always had my own money because I was very entrepreneurial. I sold quenepas, the little green berries known as Spanish limes. During the season, I sold twenty-five quenepas for a dime. We had a mango tree, and during the mango season, I would sell those too. I helped my mother sell her Avon products. I was always selling something. Even though we really didn't have money to spare, I had enough to indulge my love of music. I remember doing the math and figuring out, at the age of ten, that I could afford the Columbia subscription with my quenepa cash. My grandmother owned the place where the post office was located, so when my records arrived, they would call me to let me know.

When my mother offered me a wall to use for whatever I wanted in her travel agency, I figured out how to pay for more music: I sold records. I set up a wall-to-wall record stand and sold them on commission. A record guy would come over, and I would ask for two of this or three of that. I had a sense of what sold. Then I would buy my own records in English, collecting Broadway tunes from him, which I didn't sell. Nobody wanted those. I bought *Camelot* and *The Sound of Music*, which I listened to all the time. There was something special about the way they told stories with music that I found intriguing. Even in Spanish, with Puerto Rican music, my favorite songs were the ones that told stories. Melody was important, but I preferred the idea of listening to the story—even if I didn't understand 80 percent of what they were saying in English. If I thought there was an important word, I would write it out phonetically and then try to figure out the meaning later. There were always a couple of people in the town who spoke English, including my girlfriend from Chicago. Sometimes she would listen to the record and tell me the story. As I grew older, I loved Puerto Rican protest music. But my first love was show tunes.

That music was a natural development from my obsession with going to the movies. In my town of Vega Alta, I just had to walk three buildings over, and I was in movie heaven. They were not always age-appropriate movies. I was totally grossed out by *Ben-Hur*. I was just a kid when I saw *Psycho*, and I couldn't sleep for days. I didn't care what the movie was or whether I went alone.

Sundays at the movies were different. I went with my dad and we would see a new movie in San Juan—usually the Westerns that my dad loved so much. But when I got tired of seeing every John Wayne movie, he would let me watch my favorite movie: *The Sound of Music*. I watched it week after week after week as a kid. I watched it eighty times, without exaggeration. As an adult, before on-demand and streaming video, I made my family watch it with me every holiday when it was shown on TV. Why did an Alpine family story from World War II speak to me as a child in Puerto Rico? First, it was like the Spanish soap operas. I love a telenovela where the woman who takes care of the kids marries the son of the owner and makes the rich lady mad. These are the stories where poor people can escape their own circumstances, and *The Sound of Music* has some of that. Second, I love Captain von Trapp's convictions—that they will never give in to Hitler and the Nazis. I look forward to that scene of them escaping and singing all those beautiful songs as they leave. I love the movie's joy. It gave me the same feelings as *The Unsinkable Molly Brown*, which I watched around the same time in the same place. It was my fantasy: a poor kid makes it big, proving that it was possible to change your circumstances.

My feelings toward these two movies are intense and intertwined, and they have stayed with me. I traveled to Vermont to stay in the Trapp Family Lodge. I was fascinated by what they had done to start a new life. I purchased a couple of the records they had made in real life and read everything there was to read about them. To this day, if a new book is written about the Trapps, Lin-Manuel will give it to me as a birthday or Christmas present. On my first trip to Salzburg, I convinced the family to record a video of "Do-Re-Me."

My feelings about Julie Andrews were more complex. She came to see *Hamilton* on Broadway, but nobody told me until afterward. I was so upset with Lin-Manuel.

"Every Christmas, we watch *The Sound of Music*, and it didn't occur to you in the intermission to tell me that Julie Andrews was in the house?"

"You're going to meet her another time," he assured me. "Don't be mad that we didn't call you to be here at the end of the show to meet her."

"People call me all the time when they know there's someone I want to meet. And there's not that many people I want to meet," I said.

He was correct. A year or two later, Lin-Manuel was invited to the White House to celebrate the Kennedy Center honorees, including the legendary Rita Moreno. The organizers asked me if I wanted to sit next to Nancy Pelosi or Julie Andrews. It was not a fair question! On one hand, there was my political idol, Nancy Pelosi. On the other, there was the star of the movie I had watched more than any other in my life.

We left the hotel early to get good seats at the White House, as if we were going to a school production. When we arrived at the White House, they were waiting outside for us and brought us in by golf cart while many of the other guests were walking. The only other person in the golf cart was Aretha Franklin. Lin-Manuel and I looked at each other in disbelief. We were just about to enter the building when they told us to wait again. Then someone arrived in uniform with lots of medals on his chest and escorted us to the front row. Michelle Obama wanted Lin-Manuel to sit next to her. I took my seat between Lin-Manuel and, of course, Julie Andrews.

We shook hands. I didn't tell her I had watched *The Sound of Music* eighty times, although I wanted to. We talked about Rita Moreno and how fantastic she is. She told me stories about Rita. However, I couldn't talk about her own movie career because I didn't want to bring up my love-hate relationship with *Mary Poppins*.

Every time I tell the story about my feelings, Lin-Manuel tells me that nobody cares. But I do, and it's a story I love because it goes to the core of who I am: loyal.

As an eight-year-old boy, I knew that Julie Andrews had played in *My Fair Lady* on Broadway. But when they made the movie with Rex Harrison, the producers felt that she wasn't famous enough, so they cast Audrey Hepburn instead. Hepburn couldn't sing, so they dubbed her voice. To make up for this indignity, Disney hired Andrews to play Mary Poppins, and she was then nominated for an Oscar. That was the year when the Oscar should have gone to Debbie Reynolds for *The Unsinkable Molly Brown*, in my opinion. And nothing could change my mind. Julie Andrews did not deserve an Oscar for *Mary Poppins*. She deserved one for *The Sound of Music*. Debbie Reynolds was robbed of the only time she could have won an Oscar because of stupid studio politics. And she died without getting the recognition she deserved. I have lived with this story my whole life. I guess I read it in some entertainment gossip column sixty years ago. I probably embellished it, and it may not even be true, but it stuck with me to this day.

That was not my experience when I met Debbie Reynolds. It was one of the best days of my life. Lin-Manuel was performing *In the Heights* at the Pantages Theater in Los Angeles, and I had seen him there several times because the tour was then moving on to Puerto Rico. It was the first time a touring show with Equity performers was going to Puerto Rico, so I was trying to do my part. I had brought a reporter from Puerto Rico to LA to see what was heading their way. One day in LA, Lin-Manuel told me to come to the theater at the end of the show. "I have a surprise for you," he said.

We got in a car with the Pantages general manager and drove half an hour to the manager's friend. I had no idea whom I was going to meet. To my astonishment, it was Debbie Reynolds. I thought I was going to die. It felt so intimate, a handful of us together with the legendary Debbie Reynolds. I told her about my fascination with her and *The Unsinkable Molly Brown*. Lin-Manuel joked to her that I was the president of the Debbie Reynolds Fan Club in Puerto Rico, which had a membership of one. But it was true that I was a huge admirer. For years, I cut all the clippings I could find about her in the newspapers. A friend of mine helped me write a letter in English that I sent to her with all of those clippings. She replied to me, saying how much she had enjoyed reading them. I treasured that letter so much that I could close my eyes and picture it in my head. Somehow the letter got lost when my parents moved, and I never forgave them for it. To this day, it's because of Debbie Reynolds that we personally answer every letter that Lin-Manuel receives. People think we're crazy because so many others farm that work out. But we have two staff members who work with Lin-Manuel to answer every letter. If Debbie Reynolds could answer me personally and talk about the clippings, then Lin-Manuel could surely do the same for his fans.

We had an incredible night together. We arrived at 11:00 p.m. and stayed up talking until 2:00 a.m. If Lin-Manuel hadn't needed to perform again the next day, we would have talked until sunrise.

———

I LOVED NEW YORK'S THEATERS WELL BEFORE I HAD ENOUGH money to enjoy them. Soon after arriving in Manhattan, I would go to see the double-feature movies on Forty-Second Street because they were more affordable. Then I would walk around the corner, hoping someone would give me a coupon for the cheap tickets for a musical nearby. They would give out this kind of stuff just to fill the place, and you could buy a ticket for nothing. I saw *A Chorus Line*. I saw *Evita, The Wiz,* and *Chicago*. I saw whatever was available. That was how I found the Public Theater. I was talking to a friend about how I loved all those theater cafés in Puerto Rico and how I was getting these cheap tickets in New York. And he told me I had to go to the Public Theater, which had been founded as a nonprofit cultural beacon in 1954. It was where *Hair* had premiered a decade before I arrived in the city. I went to the Public to see a groundbreaking new show, *for colored girls who have considered suicide / when the rainbow is enuf.* That show—a unique mixture of song, poetry, and dance—would go on to Broadway. Four decades later, the Public Theater would be the birthplace of *Hamilton*, and I would end up as chair of the board of trustees. But as a struggling young man with no money in Manhattan, that was an unimaginable future.

Hamilton's success was not obvious. Lin-Manuel went on vacation after *In the Heights* and told us that he knew what his next musical would be. He had read the *Hamilton* book by Ron Chernow and wanted to make a concept album just like *Jesus Christ Superstar*. It sounded insane to me, so the following week, I bought the book and read most of it on a trip to LA. I knew very little about Alexander Hamilton other than that he was Treasury secretary at the start of the Republic, was close to Washington, and died in a duel. I quickly realized why Lin-Manuel was so fascinated. It doesn't feel like a history book. It feels like gossip you're learning from the era of the founding fathers.

I didn't realize how successful the new musical would be until Lin-Manuel performed at the White House in 2009. David Axelrod, President Obama's political strategist, had called me to ask if Lin-Manuel would perform something from *In the Heights* at an event hosted by First Lady Michelle Obama. I knew Axelrod from working together on the Freddy Ferrer campaigns. The plan was to play one of the *In the Heights* songs. But Lin-Manuel had different ideas: he wanted to sing the first song from *Hamilton*— the only song he had written so far. He sent the lyrics, and they loved the song so much that they asked him to close the show. You could just see people's reactions. I thought that even if nobody else enjoyed it, people like me—who love politics—were going to love this musical.

It took another six years for *Hamilton* to open, and over the years, I watched different audiences in different places share the same reaction. At Vassar's Powerhouse program in upstate New York. At the Public Theater in Manhattan. One night, early on at the Public, Luz and I found ourselves sitting behind Paul McCartney. It took about thirty seconds into the intermission for my wife to tell everyone that our son had written the show. McCartney turned to us and told us it was amazing. But he also said he was astonished at how hard it had been for him to get two tickets. "I'm Paul McCartney, and I couldn't get tickets," he joked. I was even more astonished that one of the biggest stars in the universe couldn't get tickets to a show where my son—the son of Puerto Rican migrants—was telling the story of the making of this country. This is the beauty of this country, I thought: a brand-new group of people can come, and their kids can be successful telling the world about the birth of the nation in an entirely new way.

Those moments sealed it for me. I decided we needed to be fully involved as investors when the producers tried to raise $12 million to move the show to Broadway. I committed to the producer Jeffrey Seller to raise 20 percent of that amount between ourselves and our friends. Luz and I wanted to invest, but we didn't have cash lying around. So we made the best decision of our lives: we mortgaged our home—the only real asset we owned—and didn't tell Lin-Manuel. He wasn't happy when he found out, but it was too late for him to stop us. In our gut, Luz and I knew it was going to be a hit. I knew enough about the business to understand what was happening. It felt no different from the gut feeling I had when I took the job with Ed Koch or when I bet it all to try to make Freddy mayor or to purchase the building for the Amber school.

———

As I've mentioned, politics was never Lin-Manuel's cup of tea. But my daughter, Cita, was far more persuadable to help with one campaign or another. When you're an adolescent, you do mundane things like collecting signatures to get someone on the ballot on a street corner at 6:00 a.m. Which was basically what they did. Lin-Manuel preferred reading books or writing. When we were trying to get Latinos elected to the school board in Washington Heights, my kids would just be there in community meetings. Later Cita accompanied me to social functions and sat through plenty of dinners across the city. Lin-Manuel never liked these events, but he did find his own way to help. As he grew older, I would hire him to write jingles for our campaigns and commercials. I used to pay him $1,000, which was probably a little over the market rate for someone who had no credits under his belt. He created jingles for the Sharpton campaign for president and Freddy for mayor, as well as smaller campaigns for the New York City Council. He was very good at jingles. You just needed to tell him a bit about the mood we were going after and which instruments made most sense. Then he would argue with you: that if you really wanted to go for that mood, you needed a trumpet. Or if this was going on Spanish radio, it needed to be more peppy. Or if we were going negative—and we did plenty of negative commercials—then let's make sure it's a bit of a horror show. He continued to work on these jingles even after he was a Tony Award winner for *In the Heights*. At that earlier stage of his career, it helped him pay the rent. It was only after *Hamilton* that he retired from writing jingles. But in the back of my mind, I always told myself that if his theater work ever went south, he could always fall back on writing jingles. Just like Charlie Sheen's character in *Two and a Half Men*.

Today Lin-Manuel gets directly involved in politics when it's very important. He has headlined fundraisers for Letitia James, the New York attorney general, because she's not just a friend; she's important for saving democracy, suing the Trump organization and the National

Rifle Association. He helped raise money for a campaign to elect the first Puerto Rican woman district attorney in the country, Deborah Gonzalez in Athens, Georgia. He helped raise money for Chuck Schumer, not just because he was my first client and is our senator but because he also fought for Broadway to get financial support to reopen after the pandemic. He understood the importance of doing commercials to get Puerto Ricans to vote in Florida. But I also know that we can never overexpose him in politics. There are many times when he just prefers to stay in the artistic lane, such as when he was promoting *Encanto*, *In the Heights*, and *tick, tick . . . BOOM!*—all in the same year. We knew that there would be no politics at that time.

We've been able, as a family, to develop a dance ensemble where everyone knows when it's time for a solo and when it's time to stay in the background. Lin-Manuel supported his mom when she joined the board of Planned Parenthood soon after Trump became president. It was important for her to raise money to be more than just a Latina on the board, so Lin-Manuel headlined a fundraiser to support her passion to advance reproductive rights.

We have hired a team of people who lead with love. Key to our team are Owen Panettieri and Sara Elisa Miller. Both were Lin-Manuel's classmates at Wesleyan. Sara choreographed the first production of *In the Heights*, and Owen played Pontius Pilate in Wesleyan's *Jesus Christ Superstar*. I can't imagine this business without them, or John Buzzetti, who is Lin-Manuel's agent. My son met John while *In the Heights* was playing and loved him.

Nobody cares more about Lin-Manuel's public image than I do. I'm never going to pull him into something that isn't important or where he can't bring something unique. The culture wars are getting worse. But some things—such as LGBTQ+ and abortion or immigrant rights and the assaults on tackling the climate crisis—are too important to stay on the sidelines. If we don't do everything we can, what's the point of having resources or a platform?

As much as we understand the power of Lin-Manuel's work and the family name, we know the purpose of our political work. It is always about something bigger than a name or fame. That was why we agreed to take part in Viva Broadway. There are so few Latinos in theater that the Broadway League asked us to help increase the number of Latinos on Broadway.

This was not a new mission for our family. Back when I was still at the Hispanic Federation, we incubated the Northern Manhattan Arts Alliance with funds from the Upper Manhattan Empowerment Zone. We argued that the arts were an economic engine and that more and more artists were moving up to our neighborhoods as the rest of the city was being gentrified. Harlem had the Apollo and other iconic Black institutions, but we had none in Washington Heights and Inwood. Now the Northern Manhattan Arts Alliance supports artists with small grants as they put together their exhibitions or begin to sell their art, and it strengthens local arts organizations. It continues to support smaller institutions and collectives of artists. It pays the rent for spaces where artists can rehearse, paint, or write. It's not sexy, but it is vital. And it was the precursor to our new campaign to help the People's Theater Project open the first off-Broadway theater uptown.

It's important in our neighborhood, and it's important on our biggest stages. I agreed to chair Viva Broadway, and we all agree with its goals. But until there's more Latino content on Broadway and we fill those stages with our faces, there will not be an increase in Latino audiences. For all Lin-Manuel's success, we still have not achieved enough for Latinos in our corner of culture and the arts.

CHAPTER 9

Maria

WE HAD BEEN FOLLOWING THE PATHS OF THE HURRICANES as they came over the horizon in September 2017. First Irma, then Maria, in quick succession. We were already making plans to take *Hamilton* to Puerto Rico, two years after it had moved to Broadway. And my family continues to live in Vega Alta, in the north. Irma left its destruction to the east and spared most of the rest of the archipelago. But when the monstrously large Maria made landfall, as a category 5 hurricane with winds of 175 miles per hour, there was no escape. There was just radio silence.

The first person I could reach was Ender Vega from my hometown, who would later be our local producer for *Hamilton*. We saw photos of my brother posted online, working on relief efforts the day after Maria passed. But we still didn't know exactly what had happened. All we had seen were the aerial photos where the bright lights of the urban areas were now extinguished.

The day Maria hit, I met with José Calderón, then president of the Hispanic Federation, and we began to plan the work we needed to do in Puerto Rico. Without knowing the facts, we already grasped that it was terrible. We began collecting donations through the Federation and talked to Mayor De Blasio. He responded by opening up all the city's firehouses to accept donations for Puerto Rico. Lin-Manuel was in Austria with his family and began writing a song to raise funds and awareness: "Almost Like Praying." I opened an account at the credit co-op in Vega Alta—the small bank that my grandfather had founded and my dad once managed—so that we could transfer funds to support the community.

Two days after Maria, we had already organized a private plane to take city parks workers from New York to Puerto Rico. They were specialists in dealing with downed electrical wires and fallen trees. Council speaker Melissa Mark Viverito was also on board. However, their plane was diverted to North Carolina while en route to San Juan as the Federal Emergency Management Agency (FEMA) took control of the airport.

By the next day, three days after the hurricane, we had made contact with my family. My brother, Elvin, told me that the place was no longer the same. "Everything is gone," he said. "Our parents' home is gone." Most of the homes in Vega Alta had lost their roofs, even if they were standing. Our parents' place was not one of them. They had built a wooden house on the edge of the town after I moved to New York. All that was left of it were the bathroom and kitchen walls, which were made of concrete. Everything else had been destroyed. My sister, Yamilla, had been living there, but she had wisely crossed the street to shelter with our brother in his concrete home as the storm arrived. They survived unharmed, watching Maria destroy our parents' home from the other side of the road (our parents had passed away by this time). My sister soon moved to a home I had just bought in nearby Dorado, where power took only a month or two to come back—unlike the rest of the islands, which suffered in darkness for months on end.

Lin-Manuel returned from Austria to help Puerto Rico, and we were soon on our way to see the situation for ourselves. It looked like a fire had razed everything. There was not a leaf on the trees. It looked like Inwood Park in my neighborhood in the depths of winter—except you knew there had never been winter in Puerto Rico. It was a couple of weeks after Maria, and there was still debris everywhere. We stayed in a hotel overrun by FEMA officials as we tried to figure out how we could help.

I'm very leery of politics in Puerto Rico and deeply suspicious about who will keep what. The Hispanic Federation leadership and my family made a quick decision on that trip that we would not work through central government channels. We visited towns and talked to mayors and community organizations to see what was needed. Then we figured out the mechanisms for delivering support through the Hispanic Federation. One of the first things we did was to stop the New York mayor from collecting any more donations. It made no sense to send water to the archipelago, for example. We talked to the people at local distributors and realized there were all sorts of supplies in Puerto Rico. We started buying locally, cutting out the middleman and all those transport costs. Instead of sending food and water, we needed to send money directly to Puerto Rico.

That was how we met chef José Andrés, who called me out of the blue to ask for help as his organization, World Central Kitchen, started his massive operation to feed Puerto Ricans.

"I don't have money," he said, on the verge of tears. "Everything is going to bounce. I need $100,000 today." It was a frantic call from someone I had met just once before in my life. I called Lin-Manuel to ask for his opinion.

"Do you know him?" he asked.

"Not really," I said. "But I know he's serving food because our friends tell us that he's opening kitchens. Let's give him the $100,000."

We wired him the cash that day.

We didn't know half the characters we were dealing with, but that was how it happened. The element of trust and your gut check need to come into the picture when there's so much to be done. "If half the shit we're doing actually gets done," I explained, "it's half more than would have gotten done before."

We were now dedicated to our single goal. All we did for six months was raise money. Lin-Manuel became the face of help. It was a lot of work, but we received eighty thousand donations. We had a breakfast every week where we brought together five or six potential donors to talk about what we wanted to do in Puerto Rico. Whenever I got a call from José Andrés, I would call the donors to tell them to send the money to José's nonprofit.

People started to contact us without our doing any media announcements or outreach. Luz took a call from a midwife she had met at some conference. She said they were delivering babies across the islands, but supporting midwives was technically a violation of the law because midwives are not a licensed profession in Puerto Rico. We gave them $25,000 to continue to deliver babies anyway.

We knew that people were dying. More than three thousand Puerto Ricans died after the hurricane, as the elderly, sick, and poor were left without food, water, power, and medicine. We didn't need to see the death statistics when they finally emerged from public health officials several months later. When your family lives in a small town, you know who's dying. My mother ran the travel agency. My father ran the credit co-op. My brother was the minister of a local Protestant church. We knew everyone, and we knew people were dying.

Lin-Manuel dedicated himself to recording the song. He recorded in Miami, Los Angeles, New York, and Puerto Rico. Everybody immediately said yes, including people whom Lin-Manuel didn't really know personally. The voices were extraordinary—among them Marc Anthony, Camila Cabello, Gloria Estefan, Luis Fonsi, Jennifer Lopez, and the legendary Rita Moreno and Rubén Blades.

However, we soon realized that the song would not be the main way we raised money. It was the generosity of everyday people who donated millions of dollars. It was so intense that we never had enough volunteers to open the mountain of letters that arrived at the Hispanic Federation every day with cash and checks. People would send a $10 bill in honor of *Hamilton*. The song raised awareness, for sure, and a few hundred thousand dollars. But the small donations amounted to millions of dollars.

———

WE REALIZED EARLY ON THAT THE ARCHIPELAGO'S GOVERNMENT was what we feared: not very effective under the shackles of colonialism and the constraints of island politics in a place of unresolved status. We also knew through our experience with the Hispanic Federation that the independent sector was the best way to effect change. There was a network of nonprofits, but they were undercapitalized. So we set about investing in nonprofits in Puerto Rico to bring them together to provide services. We didn't need to create institutions or civic leaders: the leaders were already there, experts in what was going on across Puerto Rico, with years of experience under their belt. All we needed to do was provide resources. We had done it before, in the 1990s, when we had developed the Hispanic Federation. We could do it again.

We weren't disaster relief specialists: we weren't trying to respond quickly and then move on to the next disaster, like chef José Andrés. Our structure was different. Our goal was to stay there and evolve with our partners to support whatever was needed—and whatever was needed next. It was less about responding to a crisis and more about what made sense in terms of aligning with our belief system and the needs of the archipelago.

For instance, through the midwife from Madres Ayudando Madres who contacted Luz, we connected with Profamilias, the only nonprofit abortion provider in Puerto Rico. Reproductive rights had been a focus for our family. We found that there were just five doctors, three of whom were elderly, who could perform first-trimester abortions on the islands. Since then, Luz has led a $1.3 million project to train doctors in these techniques, and nineteen have been trained since Maria.

Some of our biggest initiatives have been environmental, specifically ecotourism and coffee. For instance, we gave $1 million to the island of Culebra to restore the Flamenco Beach area after Maria's destruction. Separately, we heard through the governor that Puerto Rico's coffee crop had been wiped out. José Andrés was becoming involved with small farms, so we thought we should too. We quickly brought in what Lin-Manuel called the Coffee Avengers—Nespresso, Starbucks, and The Rockefeller

Foundation, among others. But once again, we found that the government was a barrier to helping the archipelago. Starbucks donated one million coffee seedlings, and we needed government help to accept them because coffee is highly regulated in Puerto Rico. We were stunned to learn that the archipelago's secretary of agriculture let most of the seedlings wither away on a hot tarmac. We were forced to buy another million seedlings and swore never to work with the agriculture secretary again.

Despite its shaky beginnings, the coffee project has been a phenomenal success. In 2022, Puerto Rico produced more coffee than it had the year before Maria. Just as importantly, we helped a community build itself among hundreds of small coffee growers.

However, the project we feel most connected to is the one that has transformed support for the arts in Puerto Rico. At the height of our response to Maria, I received a random email from a man named Vadim Nikitine at six in the morning. He said he had heard that we were involved in Puerto Rico and asked to talk. Since we were both up early that day, I suggested that we talk right away. So at 6:15 a.m., I learned that he had been raised in Puerto Rico, lived in Washington, DC, and had made his fortune in real estate. He had already created a foundation, called the Flamboyan Foundation, and it sounded just like what we wanted to do. We had no desire to repeat someone else's efforts. Besides, he sounded genuine, and I have always been a good judge of character. I then met his wife, Kristin Ehrgood, who ran the foundation.

Together, we created an arts fund in his foundation that has since supported arts across Puerto Rico to the tune of more than $23 million, including large donations from other foundations and the $15 million profits from the Puerto Rico performances of a show called *Hamilton*.

———

THE YEAR OF HURRICANE MARIA WAS A MATTER OF LIFE AND death for me. I had not been feeling well since the start of the year, but I dismissed the odd sensation out of hand. I'd had a medical stress test, including a full scan of my heart, and I felt that I was covered. At the time, I was traveling to London frequently because Lin-Manuel was there filming *Mary Poppins Returns*. I would go every couple of months to see him and have him review and sign fan letters. Luz called me while I was in London and told me the doctor's letter had arrived. The news was Trump-like in its zeal: I had the best heart in America.

Still, I didn't feel great. When I returned from London after just a couple of days across the Atlantic, I didn't feel totally myself. I felt enough pain that I went to the emergency room, but it was packed. As soon as I started feeling fine, I walked out without completing all the tests. The following morning, while I was driving Miguel to school, I realized that something wasn't right. I called my doctor, and he told me to go straight to the ER. It took me a little time to arrive because I hate paying for parking. I just think it's ridiculous that they charge $50 to park a car for two hours. So I drove around for a while looking for space on a street with alternate-side parking for street cleaning.

I was a couple of blocks away from the hospital, and the pain was getting worse. It wasn't really in my heart; it was all along one side, from my teeth all the way down. It was acute, and I knew that something bad was happening. I walked into the ER and announced that I was having a heart attack. They took me away, and the first thing I remember asking was "Am I going to be done by 11? Because that's when alternate-side parking is up. I have to go move my car."

People looked at me like I was a fucking nut.

I had other ideas. While I was having the heart attack, I remember thinking, "Today cannot be my day to die. Miguel is in high school. I still have six more years of parenting until this kid graduates from college. Today cannot be the day I die. Cita and Lin-Manuel have lives that are complete. They would miss me, but Miguel needs me."

The doctors told me they were taking me into surgery that same day. They wanted to put two stents into me, and I made the stupid decision to stay conscious in the operating room. I will never do that again. Big mistake. They started talking about me like a piece of meat about to be processed and stuffed into a mondongo—a tripe soup. At some point, the doctor declared that the blockage was big.

"Hey, I'm up here," I complained.

"I gave you the option, and you didn't take it," he replied.

The lack of control almost killed me more quickly than the heart attack. After the surgery, they told me not to move for six hours. I can be still for six hours—as long as you don't tell me that I can't move for six hours. I remember lying in bed with the clock opposite me, watching every minute pass by, because I couldn't get my mind away from the six hours. I was constantly looking at the clock to see when the time was up. And when the six hours were up, all I could hear in my head was *boom*.

I stood up and promptly passed out.

Even when you have a massage, they tell you to get up slowly. After surgery, that's even better advice. Instead, I got up like the house was on fire. As it happens, I have been passing out all my life. I have coped with a vasovagal nerve problem ever since I was a boy. I know when I'm going to pass out and usually have a little warning so that I can alert people around me: "I'm about to pass out. Please don't freak out. I'll be back." The last time it happened, I was on a plane to Chicago with Luz for the opening of *The Cher Show*. I asked her to tell the flight attendant, and I just about heard them asking if they needed to divert the plane. Luz told them I would be fine.

However, by this time in the hospital, six hours after my surgery, Luz had already left. My friends Lorraine and her husband Louis were there, and as I passed out, I heard her screaming, "He's passing out! Is it another heart attack? Oh my God!" She was freaking out, and all I could think was that I wished I could tell her I'd be back in a couple of seconds. She created such a drama that they made me stay in the hospital an extra day.

"Because of you, I'm staying longer than I need to," I told her, ungrateful as ever. "This has happened to me since I was nine years old. There was no reason to create the melodrama you did."

I was forced to grow accustomed to less control over many aspects of my life. I began eating very differently. I stopped eating most Puerto Rican food. I stopped eating rice every day of my life. I stopped eating bread, processed food, and lots of carbs. Those are now treats. Once a month, I need to have white rice with fried eggs, sunny side up with ketchup. I dropped most meat, eating it only once a month. I eat lots of things I don't like. There's nothing I hate more than kale. I now eat kale and then I feel like I need to take a nap because my mouth gets so tired of chewing. If I was supposed to eat salad, God would have made me a rabbit. Not eating Puerto Rican food every day is horrendous. But it allows me to keep going.

I took cardiac rehab very seriously. I had to do it twice a week, so I made sure to go four times a week. It's like everything in my life. I don't know what moderation means. Three months after the surgery, I had recovered from a lot of the artery issues that I had been suffering. To this day, if I can walk somewhere, I will walk everywhere. I love to walk in New York City—and, quite frankly, anywhere that is not Los Angeles. But I hate exercising in place. You won't get me on an exercise bike. Using a machine that goes nowhere is the stupidest thing anybody has invented. At least the cardio rehab was interesting because I had all those cables hanging from me. The idea of looking at a screen while walking in place is just hell.

During the pandemic, I took long walks in the park across the street from our house. Those walks were the highlight of my day. It was hilly, and I could go up and down all the way to the river on the other side and back.

Today my health is good, and my heart is fine. My doctor, Dr. Dmitry Feldman, is fantastic, and I see him every six months. I do the stress tests every year, and I keep pushing them to test me more—to push me harder and get the tests done more quickly.

I am a great patient. My family says I'm not, but they are wrong. They say I'm a horrible patient because I have an accelerated life. But if I didn't have this life, I might as well be dead. I'm not going to change because I don't sleep enough. I wish I could sleep more. Really. I sleep four or five hours a night, and I used to sleep three hours. So it's getting better by their standards. I eat well. I exercise. I have coffee as often as I miss it. Some days, that's maybe four cups. Other days, it's maybe eight. Sometimes at 11:00 p.m., when I'm about to watch the news, I want to have a coffee, so I'll make myself a cup. I fall asleep whenever my body is ready to go to sleep. Sleeping doesn't make me feel better. I feel the same whether I sleep more or less. What I eat during the day has more to do with how I feel. If I eat shitty food, I feel shittier at night.

That's why I know that even if I don't like the food that God said I must eat now, I will eat it.

As I said, I'm a great patient.

———

WHAT WE KNOW, ABOVE ALL, IS THE POWER OF ARTS AND CUL-ture. That was why it was such a priority for us to take *Hamilton* to Puerto Rico after Maria. Lin-Manuel had taken *In the Heights* to Puerto Rico and had been determined to do the same with *Hamilton* well before Maria. For reasons I can't fully explain, our children have an unbelievable connection to Puerto Rico. That's not normal for second-generation kids; it's way deeper than anything I've seen in that generation. However, taking *Hamilton* to Puerto Rico was a real challenge. This was the first time the show had gone on tour, and it was headed to San Francisco after that. I wanted to take the show to the University of Puerto Rico, but the hurricane had damaged the theater extensively. We raised $1 million to repair the place, and I was traveling back and forth every two weeks to make sure the construction was on track.

The first week of December, I was back home when I received a letter from the union of the University of Puerto Rico. They wrote to Lin-Manuel to let us know they were going on strike and would picket *Hamilton* when it opened. We were a union production, and there was no way we were crossing a picket line. Moreover, the university union was making demands that were simple and just. The university wanted to eliminate the long-standing benefit that the children of employees didn't have to pay tuition at the university. So I went to Puerto Rico, met with the union, and told them there was no way around it: we wouldn't bring the show to Puerto Rico. I started saying publicly that the show wasn't coming, and it made the news. I delivered the news in an amicable way, but I was a bit in your face. As it became clearer that it wasn't going to happen at the university, we started inquiring about the Centro de Bellas Artes, where we had taken *In the Heights*.

There was no warning for the people involved. Everybody was still getting ready for the university stage—in fact, they were proud that the set installation was ahead of schedule. Just before Christmas, we broke the news that we were switching theaters. It was a huge undertaking to move with less than two weeks to opening. But in the end, it delayed the opening by just three days. There were only three days of rehearsal and one day of preview. For a new tour, on a new stage, it was no time at all.

Despite all the headaches, that show really changed the mood of Puerto Rico. At Lin-Manuel's insistence, one-quarter of the tickets were priced at $10, and you had to show proof that you lived on the archipelago to buy them. Those tickets gave ten thousand Puerto Ricans the chance to experience something they never could have expected otherwise. We would time the standing ovations when Lin-Manuel first walked on stage, and each one would run for one to two minutes. That's unbelievably long for anyone and any performance. The show became something that normal people talked about. And it brought tourists over: the hotels were full again. We were in the media every single day, promoting the show and the arts. It was not only a very intense experience but also intensely impactful.

It was so intense that Lin-Manuel was not allowed to do anything else because he couldn't afford to get sick. "Dad, I'm not going to get sick," he would tell me. "Don't worry about this."

"But on Broadway, you were doing seven shows, and your alternate did one," I said. "Do you want to do that?"

"No, Dad," he said. "I'm going to do eight shows a week."

Hamilton succeeded in every way, raising $15 million for the Flamboyan Arts Fund. Now we have such a good relationship with the private sector in Puerto Rico that we can raise money from them. Our first fundraiser from businesses in Puerto Rico raised $1 million.

I don't mind asking people for money. It's never for me. People know that I'll take care of their money to do good things. We have a water project to help with purifying water. We have a solar project with Jennifer Lopez, where we installed solar energy at the twenty federally qualified health centers in Puerto Rico, so when Hurricane Fiona hit in 2022, those clinics didn't lose power. When there were major earthquakes in Puerto Rico in 2020, we were able to mobilize quickly and open help centers through our network of organizations. We never worked with government, so we could be transparent with people about how we were spending their money. We have now reached the point where the federal government goes to the Hispanic Federation to provide money for particular projects in Puerto Rico.

Nothing will ever replace the lost lives and suffering of Hurricane Maria and the reckless mistakes of the recovery. However, we have rebuilt with stronger foundations. My parents' old home is now made of concrete. The archipelago's nonprofits are a network with years of investment behind them. Our coffee farmers are a thriving community. Women's health care is better than it was before the hurricane. And our artists have support that is entirely new. Puerto Rico may still be struggling with political instability and crippling debt, but the Puerto Rican people there and in diaspora communities draw on deep levels of talent and strength to survive and thrive.

CHAPTER 10

Change Is Constant

MY JOURNEY AS A PUERTO RICAN IN NEW YORK IS BOTH intensely personal and entirely representative of Latinos across the United States. We have firmly rooted identities that are in flux as we travel through our American lives. There is no single Latino community, and this makes it hard for political and business experts to generalize and strategize about the fastest-growing demographic group in this country. At the same time, each part of the Latino community is itself evolving as American values and experiences change our sense of place and culture. We don't represent a Spanish-speaking version of the African American experience, even as many of us live with the suffering and scars of persistent racism. There is community in our shared Latino identity, as well as intense rivalry.

Our immigration history is complex. I didn't register as a voter for several elections because I was so preoccupied with the politics of the place I had called home. It took me time to understand how the politics back home related to my experiences here—and I am obviously much more political than most people. My journey is not unusual. We see people getting involved in school boards and other aspects of government that shape their own experiences. But each community tries to insert itself into a country that is in a different place every time a new wave of immigrants arrives. Over the course of the last two generations, Mexican Americans saw large numbers of Puerto Ricans arrive, followed by Cubans and then Dominicans. Over the last several years, they have been joined by Central Americans and Venezuelans.

To understand those Latino communities, you need to understand not just where they have come from but what their country faced when that wave of immigration happened. You need to understand how that community relates to the others who were here before. If you don't spend the time to engage with how and why they left or what happened when they arrived, you cannot create a coherent political message for such a diverse group.

Take the Freddy Ferrer campaign for New York mayor in 2001 and compare it to Antonio Villaraigosa's campaign for Los Angeles mayor just four years later. They succeeded in Los Angeles where we failed. Antonio was the rising star, where Freddy was more of the underdog. Still, the reality is that LA is overwhelmingly Latino, while in New York, we were dealing with maybe 20 percent of the population and 18 percent of the vote. In LA, the culture is dominated by Mexican Americans. But New York Latino voters are majority Puerto Rican with a large chunk of Dominicans. We had to convince the Dominicans that a Puerto Rican could represent them, building a sense of Latinidad along the way. In LA, the journey was much simpler because the Latino electorate was more uniform and more concentrated, so they had to jump through fewer hoops. Both candidates came from the dominant Latino group; it would have been even harder for us if Freddy had been Dominican. But our Latino diversity in New York has made it that much harder to elect our first Latino mayor. Today, our Latino community in New York includes a much larger Colombian population, Ecuadorians, and Mexicans. Our conditions continue to change, while in Los Angeles, the electorate is similar to what it was when Villaraigosa was elected. We need to constantly figure out how we can connect with this changing community.

You cannot even talk about one Puerto Rican community anymore. Puerto Ricans have migrated to Florida. In New York, we are into our second and third generation of the Puerto Rican community. We grew up with the African American community in the city, and many of the few conservatives among us moved to New Jersey. In Florida, the culture mixed with Cuban Americans. In New York, we mixed with Dominicans. And in San Juan itself, people watch cable TV now, so NBC is as popular as the local WAPA station. In one generation, the culture has changed from the way it was when I left Puerto Rico. So you have a generation that is going to Florida that is already more American than the earlier generation that moved to New York. They already understand the terms "Democrats" and "Republicans." It's a mindset that exists in Puerto Rico in ways that it didn't in the 1950s and 1960s, when the first generation came over. The population is more affluent, and the connection between the archipelago and the mainland is closer, with a constant back-and-forth.

This dispersion of the Puerto Rican population has had profound consequences in terms of our nation's politics. In the New York area, we remain the second-largest group in the city. But we are also in Westchester and Yonkers. We crossed the bridge and entered what used to be Cuban neighborhoods. We went to Long Island, especially those who were better off. Puerto Ricans no longer automatically fly to New York or Chicago before going somewhere else. Now Puerto Ricans are flying to Ohio or Georgia or Texas. We are flying to Florida, where there are now more than one million Puerto Ricans. And in each of those hubs, Puerto Ricans began to look at other possibilities. As a result, many Puerto Rican Floridians moved to Georgia, especially in and around the Atlanta area. Some ended up in Texas, and now there are larger Puerto Rican populations in Dallas and Houston. More cosmopolitan cities ended up with a greater Puerto Rican community. There are even Puerto Rican communities in Alaska, which grew after the island started developing oil refineries in the 1960s and 1970s. When Alaska started building its own refineries, the managers came to Puerto Rico to recruit new workers. Puerto Ricans moved with employment—especially for jobs that paid well above average. People like my nieces and nephews in Puerto Rico have a choice of making $20 an hour as a full medical doctor on the islands or moving to Florida to see a significant jump in salary. Staying in Puerto Rico is much more of a cultural and political statement than an economic imperative—because the latter would lead you to take the first plane to the mainland.

Those choices became painfully clear as Puerto Rico plunged into the fiscal crisis, along with an ocean of debt, in 2014. I was friendly at the time with Governor Padilla, who was a big

Hamilton fan, and we used to talk about what the crisis meant for the archipelago. At the same time, President Obama's Treasury team reached out to Lin-Manuel and me, asking us to support a plan for Puerto Rico to be able to declare bankruptcy. The way previous governors had negotiated with hedge funds, these outside investors could actually reach into the government's bank account and seize the money needed to run the government. They were the first in line to get the money. The only way to stop that was to declare bankruptcy, but that wasn't an option for Puerto Rico as a territory—in contrast to a city such as Detroit.

The Obama administration had very few options to help as they negotiated with a Republican Congress. Finally they created a fiscal control board, or la junta, like a military dictatorship—a plan known as the Puerto Rico Oversight, Management and Economic Stability Act (Promesa). There was real pain. Many people in Puerto Rico did not agree. But I had lived through the fiscal control board in New York, and I knew it had created the conditions that had allowed the city to emerge from bankruptcy. Most of the Obama officials felt it was the only way to stop the total ruin of Puerto Rico. So we supported it.

There have been real consequences. What makes me the saddest are the cuts to the university and the wider public education system that taught me so much. However, I have been an executive several times in my life, and I know there's always an opportunity to cut fat. There are always things that you want to do that won't be possible now. They may need to come later, and that isn't fair. I wasn't in Puerto Rico to live with the consequences of Promesa, but I was in New York to live with the consequences of its fiscal control board. If there had been another option, we would have fought for it. Could we have stayed silent? Yes, we could. Many did. Others criticized it without offering an alternative solution. But this was too important for Puerto Rico.

I still get picketed and heckled for my position. People on the left interrupt me when I talk to protest against my support for Promesa. When they heckle me, I heckle back. The ultraleft is as bad as the ultraright. I just happen to often agree with the ultraleft and not at all with the ultraright. But I still think they live in la-la land. Half of the shit they want to do will not work in real life. The ideal world is not the world in which I live. I live in a world where you have to make decisions, and some decisions are imperfect. Still, in my estimation, they are better than doing nothing. If we're ever to get to where I hope we will, which is a soaring nation that joins the rest of Latin America, Puerto Rico will have to be fiscally solvent.

As for politics in Puerto Rico today, it's hard to feel optimistic. As much as the United States has created progress, it has also damaged the archipelago. For example, there are more roads and cars in Puerto Rico today than ever before. The only things that exist in greater numbers than cars are perhaps guns. This is an island that you could drive around, in its entirety, in one day. What we needed to spend money on was mass transport, which is how people should be moving from one place to another. Instead, the funding available from the United States was for road construction and repairs. We could have invested less in buildings with air conditioning and more on architecture that took advantage of the wind that comes from the entire northern corridor of the island. But it's all too late now. All those things that represent progress often represent the wrong kind of progress.

That was true after Hurricane Maria too. The more we asked for help, the more we brought statehood to the archipelago. We embraced a mentality of expecting handouts, and it's hard to quit that habit. When my uncle founded the Puerto Rican Independence Party, it was the second party in the islands in the early 1950s. They elected a ton of representatives to the lower house. Today, our so-called progress has accelerated statehood to the degree that there's an entire generation in Puerto Rico who cherish and are proud of their US citizenship. I'm not sure how to fix Puerto Rico. Perhaps I'm too old to figure it out. In any case, something needs to happen to determine the archipelago's political status, because that lies at the root of the problem.

What we need is a referendum in Puerto Rico where Congress actually listens to and implements the will of the people.

———

THE PUERTO RICAN COMMUNITY IN THE UNITED STATES doesn't have a large middle class. When people moved to Long Island or Yonkers, they hoped to build a better life—maybe to buy a little house. Instead, they continue to be poor in these other neighborhoods that are more affordable than the big city. That accounts for some of the appeal of someone like Donald Trump. In the case of Puerto Ricans, the root cause is that educational attainment continues to lag behind that of the general population. The labor market became more competitive, and higher wages depended on higher education than people had needed in the past.

Part of the reason for that lack of education is a failure of policy. As much as people needed public aid, they also needed incentives to study so that they could secure better jobs. When we were doing our research at the Hispanic Federation through the 1990s, it was clear that a common denominator for all Latinos was feeling disconnected from the mainstream economy. When you asked them about the number one problem facing our community, discrimination was up there with education and employment. You might have expected Puerto Ricans—as U.S. citizens with deep roots in the country—to feel less of that. But they did not, and they were justified in this feeling.

The Republican Party was moving sharply to the right during those years as Newt Gingrich grew in stature and power. Immigration reform—which was a historic event under Ronald Reagan—became unacceptable. And the path to Donald Trump's open hatred of immigrants became clear. When people talk about discrimination, they are feeling its impact on education, employment, and across the culture.

At the same time, studies continue to show very clearly that Latinos want to be considered on the basis of their country of origin rather than as one organized group. They want to be called Mexicans or Colombians even generationally, after the first waves of immigration. Latinos are getting closer to African Americans. They are our neighbors, and we are sharing the same experiences of poverty. What is different, clearly, is that we can return to our families' countries of origin and still feel a connection. You can continue to be treated as something else while still enjoying a full life. These are privileges that were intentionally erased for African Americans.

There is a counterweight to these feelings. The Latino community across the nation has grown more organized and supportive, regardless of where your family came from. In the early days, Puerto Ricans and Mexicans fought many battles to gain a political foothold and secure quality education and civil rights. Now, when Venezuelan families arrive at the port authorities, there is a network that includes community organizations and government support to help them. That didn't exist for Puerto Ricans: our network was made up of family members and friends. My network was my aunt who gave me a bunk bed in a room in her crowded apartment. There were no intake workers trying to find me a place to live and handing me a little bag with essentials. When I was living in Chelsea in those early days, people met in basements on weekends to play dominoes and billiards. There was a community that allowed me to hang out during these sessions where the neighborhood all came together.

There can be tensions, of course. When a community like the Puerto Rican community hasn't achieved what it could have after seventy years, there's a level of distrust of communities that arrived more recently. Even though people continue to help one another, rivalries rise to the surface. There were leaders in our community who believed that my work on the Reagan-era immigration reform would benefit Dominicans too much, which led them to question my Puerto Rican identity. They couldn't understand that organizing around common areas such as voting rights, quality education, and housing would give us all more power. Such attitudes come from a deficit mentality: that we have so little that we cannot afford to share anything or we'll be worse off. My argument was that we could achieve more if there were more of us.

Some of these tensions come from racial and class divisions. Some Dominicans talk about living "close to the border"—meaning Haiti—to explain the color of their skin. Like Dominicans, in Puerto Rico, we create seventeen different shades of color to talk around race: you're not Black, you're jabao or trigueño. There's racism among all of us, and it manifests itself in the horrific ways that racism always manifests itself, with darker-skinned people making less money, having fewer opportunities, and enduring discrimination. Still, race in the United States is measured differently and organized differently. In our countries of origin, we discriminate and pretend that we don't. In the United States, there's an entire history of organized, legalized discrimination. As Latinos become more settled, we're internalizing those racial definitions and attitudes. Add discrimination to the many basic issues that we need to address, along with inadequate housing, education, and health care.

If people want to spend their lives dealing with race among the Latino community, more power to them. If other people just want to work on colorism in our community, I will support them. But I want to spend my energy making sure there's no discrimination against anyone in our community either from within or from others, whether they are recently arrived Venezuelans or third-generation Puerto Ricans.

It's true that under the Latino umbrella, there are people who are privileged and many more who are not. We're all lumped together. If you're in a more privileged position, your job is to help those who are not. Your job is to spend your life creating opportunities for those who don't have those privileges. Those are the people I care about and the people I have spent my time working for in the community. If color gives you access to opportunity, you must use that access to help others who don't have that advantage.

However it's also true that we're changing, as Latinos, by mixing with and learning from other communities. Take the relationship between Puerto Ricans and Mexicans in the United States. We as Puerto Ricans would look at Mexicans' entertainment, their artists and their movies, as part of their very rich culture that survived centuries of Spanish and American oppression. I remember as a kid seeing the pictures in *Tesoro de la Juventud,* my favorite book, of the indigenous burial places and pyramids in Mexico. I have always had enormous respect for this culture that has survived centuries of oppression. There are high school mariachi contests starring kids of Mexican migrants, generations removed from their homeland culture, and they still have these competitions. How does that happen? Our culture has an unbelievable capacity to survive.

———

LATINOS IN THE UNITED STATES HAVE EMBARKED ON AN INCREDible journey. In 2000, we represented 35 million Americans. Two decades later, in 2021, we had grown 78 percent to 62.5 million. We are the largest driver of population growth in the country. In another two decades, by 2040, we are projected to be 87.6 million strong—well over 20 percent of the population. That growth has happened in many states where Latinos never used to settle in large numbers, according to analysis by UCLA's Latino Policy and Politics Institute. Across the South and Midwest, Latino communities have grown rapidly, even in states where the overall population declined.

At this point, two-thirds of Latinos in the United States were born here. Apart from Puerto Ricans, who were by definition born in the United States, the most Americanized Latino communities are those of Mexican and Panamanian descent. Almost three-fourths of Mexican Americans were born here, compared to around two-thirds of Panamanians. Except for very recent arrivals from Venezuela, the rest of the Latino population is divided down the middle—half were born here, half in their country of origin. That means an ever-higher proportion of Latinos who speak

English at home. One-third of Latinos say they speak only English at home; twenty years ago, it was just one-fifth. That's particularly true in Panamanian and Puerto Rican homes.

Mexican Americans still dominate the Latino population, representing more than half of our community. They are the largest Latino group in forty out of fifty states. A distant second are Puerto Ricans, followed by Salvadorans, Cubans, and Dominicans. However, that ranking misses more recent changes. While much smaller in number, Guatemalan, Honduran, Salvadoran, and Venezuelan communities have grown very rapidly—reflecting the crises those nationalities have suffered back home. Among these newcomers, South Americans have generally moved to places where Latinos were already well established. Central Americans have tended to move to the Midwest and East Coast.

Latinos are not just diverse in terms of where they come from. Different communities have different demographic profiles. While the Latino population is younger than the general population, some groups—especially South Americans and Cubans—tend to be older, with a median age in the late thirties as opposed to the late twenties. They also tend to be better educated. Mexicans, Guatemalans, and Salvadorans tend to skew toward men, while South Americans skew toward women.

Dig deeper into the economics, and you can clearly see the gap between African Americans and Latinos, as well as how that plays out in our politics. Between 2000 and 2020, the poverty rate among African Americans fell slightly, from 24 to 21 percent. Over the same period, the poverty rate among Latinos fell from 22 to 16 percent. The same trends exist for homeownership—it has been rising for Latinos and declining for African Americans. In contrast, the poverty rate among whites edged up slightly, from

8 to 9 percent—still far below the rate for communities of color. Poverty remains high among Puerto Ricans and Central Americans, compared to the lower levels for South Americans.

However, compared to the white mainstream, when the economy worsens, African Americans and Latinos remain just as vulnerable. Black and Latino families are more likely than whites to drop out of the middle class every year, according to analysis by the Pew Research Center. That was especially true during the COVID-19 pandemic. Around one in five Blacks and Latinos dropped out of the middle class between 2020 and 2021, compared with 15 percent of whites. Just 8 percent of Latinos moved up the economic ladder—from middle to upper levels—compared with 18 percent of whites during the same period. That disparity is generally true when there are no economic shocks such as a pandemic: it is easier for Blacks and Latinos to fall out of the middle class and much harder for them to move up into the upper-income levels. These patterns track closely with education levels: those who graduate with less than a high school diploma are much more likely to drop out of the middle class, and those with bachelor's degrees are much more likely to move into higher income levels. This is precisely why the fight for better education matters so much in our communities.

The same disparities are painfully obvious when you look at the toll of suffering during the pandemic. The number of cases per capita was far higher in the Latino neighborhoods of New York than in the white neighborhoods of Manhattan and Brooklyn. In Latino areas such as Corona, Elmhurst, and Jackson Heights, there was one case for every nine people. In the wealthier parts of Manhattan, it was one case for every twenty people. That translated into far higher death rates. Luz and I got chills every time we heard an ambulance siren in the neighborhood. Someone else was dying.

———

You can see these cultural shifts playing out in political battlegrounds across the country. In Florida, this has left many establishment Democrats confused. The reality isn't so complicated. For Puerto Ricans in Florida, their neighbors are less progressive and less African American than the neighbors of Puerto Ricans in New York. On gun control, we mirror the general population's belief. Hunting is important for many Latinos. We also own many small businesses, and some owners want to feel protected by having a gun. But, like most Americans, we believe that guns appropriate for wars have no place in our communities. Why do you need more than a pistol to defend yourself, or a rifle to hunt, if you actually believe in the Second Amendment?

However, the issue of abortion is different. We wrap it around the question of having control over your body or your reproductive health. But when you add the question of whether it should be legal at six weeks, or sixteen, or twenty-two, it becomes much more divisive. You begin to lose support at a faster rate than among the general population. Class is a mitigating factor: education and income change the way Latinos think about abortion for people such as my wife and my daughter. But we partly come from a culture where motherhood is key to who we are.

On top of that, Latino religious beliefs make it OK to suffer in life. It's OK to have a child if the mother doesn't want it. It's OK if a young mother can't go to college or if she is limited for the rest of her life because she had children when she wasn't ready for them. People justify all those attitudes. Religion, whether people are Pentecostal or Catholic, affects our belief about abortion. Let's always make the argument that women must have choice. It's not about abortion. It's about choice. If a woman decides to have a child, then the government needs to create housing, childcare, health care, and educational opportunities so her choice doesn't force her to be poor forever. It's also OK for a woman to have a child when she thinks her circumstances are right. Recently my company Hamilton Campaign Network commissioned a study of Latino New Yorkers. Three fourths of Latinos supported the right to choose.

Henry Cuellar, a conservative Texas Democrat who opposes abortion rights, has won close primary contests after many years in Congress. Cuellar represents a district stretching from the Rio Grande to San Antonio, and he supported Hillary Clinton for president. But in recent years, he has faced tough challenges from more progressive Democrats, such as Jessica Cisneros, whom we supported in 2022 at Latino Victory. Cisneros placed abortion at the center of the contest, and she lost by only a few hundred votes. That contest represents where we are as a community: divided fifty-fifty. For sure, abortion wasn't the only issue in the campaign or at the heart of Cisneros's appeal. Ocasio-Cortez and Sanders both campaigned for her, and they all talked much more about economic issues. Still, reproductive rights were important, and she drew strong support from outside groups such as EMILY's List and Planned Parenthood because of that. When you look at the Latinos who are won over by Republicans, the abortion debate is a clear demarcation. The irony is that countries like Mexico and Colombia in Latin America are moving toward choice through legislation—even as Latinos in the United States, including in Puerto Rico, are moving in the other direction.

That's why we should stop seeing politics in this country as black-and-white because when we do that, we miss the point that in many communities, Latinos across the country are persuadable Democrats. Not necessarily base Democrats.

The extent to which Latinos are persuadable varies across the country. We are much more persuadable in Florida than in New York, where we are base Democrats. We have to work that much harder for Puerto Ricans in Florida or Georgia. We're electing Latinos as Republicans and Democrats in Georgia, which is a purple state. How we deal with Latinos in these places needs to differ. Instead, we keep treating everyone as if they're base Democrats everywhere in the country.

In Puerto Rico itself, most of the leadership leans toward the Democrats, and we were told for a long time that Republicans were bad people. But even there, if we had a real election of just Republicans and Democrats, I think 40 percent would vote Republican. The archipelago has been moving to the right over the last few decades, and that's why numerous antiabortion bills have been introduced in the legislature, although none of them have passed. On economic issues, Puerto Rico in the 1950s was almost socialist, with 28 percent of all workers employed by the government and large companies under government control. We are running away from that today. The Catholic church, which has focused heavily on eradicating poverty, is adapting to the growth of the Pentecostal and evangelical churches. Where the Catholic church aligns with government, the Pentecostal church is much more hands-on in people's lives. People give 10 percent of their salary to the Pentecostal churches because they're so important to every element of day-to-day life. From culture to the economy to personal faith, Puerto Rican culture is shifting, and so are the politics.

What that means for Latino politics on the mainland is a greater need for understanding context and culture. Cubans and Venezuelans, who were running away from socialism and communism, arrived when the Democratic Party was in a battle between the left and the center and when the Republican Party—rightly or wrongly—was seen as conservative. All of this is happening at a time when disinformation is huge as it flows through social media instead of news traveling through newspapers, radio stations, or TV networks. More and more Latinos are getting their news through Facebook, YouTube, and WhatsApp, so the knowledge base on which we build our political assumptions is rotten half the time.

Donald Trump and his allies lie, cheat, and tell half-truths. He started his candidacy by presenting who he was. People kept saying that Trump was a hypocrite, but that's wrong. We have known him in New York City forever. He was a bigot from the very beginning, and he presented to us precisely who he was.

My psychological training has been important to help me understand this approach of establishing the essence of who we are and what we radiate about ourselves. Voters have feelings about people, which is why my partner, Roberto, talks about politics as a mixture of art and science. I want to know how my candidate relates to their family and friends because that shapes how they relate to others. It's the core of their connection to voters.

As much as I hate everything Trump stands for, I understand that voters—including Latinos, who have every reason to hate his racism and policies—like him because he's decisive and entertaining. He presents an aura that he's in charge and will take care of everyone. He doesn't fool most Latino voters, but the one-third of our voters who do like him need to be confronted with the right arguments. You need to figure out, based on their neighbors and social groups, how much to spend on reaching them to try to siphon off as many as possible. Our real target is the large chunk that is somewhere in the middle, such as the Cubans who voted for Hillary Clinton, who need to know that Joe Biden is not a socialist. Republicans don't need a majority of Latinos to win. They need to peel away just enough people in the states that are important to get the electoral votes. And we need to work hard to stop that from happening, making sure our arguments fit the bill.

What Trump revealed was the power of destructive forces in our country. We worked so hard as a diverse society to accept differences, to move beyond the division that does not move society forward. But he unleashed all the ugliness that we all carry within us. He allowed for a conversation that should never have happened because it leads to nothing good. He allowed that conversation to fester. To live in a pluralistic society, you need to allow for conversation. Instead, he told a group of people who felt attacked that somehow Black and Brown people are responsible for the fact that their kids cannot buy a house as they did. And the COVID-19 pandemic exposed how divided we are economically and racially, on top of this horrible conversation that Trump allowed to occur. That's why we need, above everything else, candidates who have a clear moral compass. It's at the heart of everything we value as a community and country.

However, we also need to be honest with ourselves so that we can be more effective when we confront Trump and the forces behind him. For a long time we have shown the video of Trump throwing paper towels at people in Puerto Rico after Hurricane Maria, through digital and TV advertising. It helped with the atmospherics in our community to say that Trump was bad and here was an example of Trump being bad. But it never touched him at the most human level. He claimed to care about the communities that were suffering from a broken economy. But when unemployment started to soar at the start of COVID-19, when our community started being hit, he was detached from what was happening. His response, along with his lack of empathy for economic misery, was far more powerful than seeing him throw paper towels in Puerto Rico.

Trump uses a fascist playbook that we have seen in Latino history in many countries. He pretends to represent the white working poor while boasting about his wealth because his supporters want to be like him. They aspire to have their name on some big building. But it's a fantasy, and it distorts everything around him. One of our nephews was explaining how the January 6 insurrection was all a misunderstanding. It just got out of hand. I have no doubt that many people went there to demonstrate peacefully. But as trials and arrests have uncovered, many went to DC to try to overthrow our government. Trump used the moment to incite a MAGA mob, to stop the count of electoral votes to support his assertions that the election had been stolen. Some are too far gone to listen to the argument, but most others are not. Latinos will listen to reason.

———

TEXAS IS A GREAT CASE STUDY IN HOW WE NEED TO TALK TO Latino communities differently depending on their context. Southern Texas is very different from San Antonio, Austin, and Dallas. The economic message can be the same across the state, but the message that must be different is about immigration. When you live at the border, you directly feel the impact of lots of people coming into your town. If the economy is fine, it's tough for Republicans to make immigration a real issue in Latino communities. At a time when there are many vacant jobs out there, it's much harder to make immigration an important issue for Latino voters than it was during the Trump years. For white communities, it's tied to racism and has less to do with the economy. Today, you need two jobs just to survive, and the real issues are inflation and low wages. As long as the political debate is about a growing economy, people have no problem voting for Democrats. If you ask Latinos what they believe, across the country, they will say that Democrats—much more than Republicans—worry more about the things they worry about. Even then, we need to adapt our economic argument to different parts of the country. Gas prices are more impactful in Texas and California than in New York City, where we don't drive as much as people do elsewhere.

In Texas, the Mexican American population is constantly being renewed with waves of migration. That's very different from other parts of the Southwest. In Arizona, the Latino population is more stable and is growing more because of childbirth rates than because there's a new wave moving in. Those dynamics have a real impact on how people behave politically.

To succeed in the border communities of Texas, Democrats need to have something else in their favor. Hillary Clinton performed better in southern Texas than Joe Biden because she is a star. She's a smart woman, married to a president whom Latinos loved, and she came across as a normal person. Her intelligence and her stardom are everything. In 2001, we found 220,000 Latino voters in New York who had only ever voted for Hillary Clinton in their whole lives. They just voted for the star. That's also part of the reason why Trump is attractive to some of these voters. He is also a star. Alexandria Ocasio-Cortez is a star. She can do a makeup tutorial on Instagram Live—and use it to explain economic issues in the simplest ways. We as Democrats will never have enough AOCs or Hillary Clintons. We have to focus on recruiting candidates who are young, who understand digital media as a direct way to communicate with voters, and who worry about how economic issues are impacting real people. We have to get Latino candidates elected so that we're represented at the table. More diversity means more power and support for everyone.

Being charismatic is not enough. You need to talk about economic issues that matter to Latinos—and you need to show that you care. Beto O'Rourke in Texas was a good case in point. And he won the Latino vote. Language is a proxy for caring. If all you do is start every Latino event by saying something in Spanish—even if you barely understand it—that's a statement that you care. Michael Bloomberg got away with this in New York because he knew that for TV, he needed to give only a ten- or fifteen-second clip of Spanish. Beto could speak much more Spanish, and it mattered. Maybe the elites in our community were upset that he wasn't in fact Latino, but he actually spoke better Spanish than many of them. He also has that rhetorical skill of speaking in crescendo, like our Latin American leaders who grab you with their rhetoric and take you with them on a journey. Because he was speaking about issues that really matter to people, explaining immigration in terms of how these people perform the jobs that we're not doing anymore, he could move Latino voters. He could explain what Republicans have failed to achieve in Texas in economic terms because they're just fighting the culture wars to get enough white voters—and maybe find enough Latinos to stop Democrats from winning.

———

LATINO COMMUNITIES ARE CHANGING ACROSS THE COUNTRY. IN the Rust Belt towns of Ohio and Pennsylvania, more and more

Dominicans are being elected to city councils and school boards. They're on the verge of breaking through to state legislatures as they build a bench of elected representation.

In Chicago, politics is even more segregated than in New York, with the Latino community split fairly evenly between Mexicans and Puerto Ricans. It used to be slightly more Puerto Rican, and now the Mexican community is bigger. But more and more, Mexicans and Puerto Ricans look alike politically—more progressive on social and economic issues. The Puerto Rican leaders in Chicago used to be far more to the left. They were even militant supporters of independence. Oscar López Rivera, the supposed leader of the FALN, grew up in Chicago. The FALN was responsible for more than 130 bomb attacks in the 1970s and 1980s, including the 1975 bombing of the Fraunces Tavern in Manhattan that killed four people. Even though he was not directly linked to any attack, López Rivera was jailed in 1981 and released only in 2017, when President Obama commuted his sentence. His brother is still a Puerto Rican community leader in Chicago and a friend. That's why Chicago is the only place in the country with two huge sculptures of Puerto Rican flags, planted in the heart of the Puerto Rican community, in Humboldt Park. The only fully fledged Puerto Rican museum in the country is there too. The city's Latino community included a very active, progressive, leftist leadership for a long time.

For the Mexican community in Chicago, immigration is also an important issue, and as Puerto Ricans intermarry with other Latinos, it has become more important to our community too. But it's never at the top of our mind. You have to ask Puerto Ricans specifically about immigration for them to say it's important.

These Latino communities are dedicated to economic and social progress for their families. They're still young enough generationally that many of our children are the first in their family to go to college. This is the litmus test for the second generation. I have grown old in Washington Heights with many Dominicans who used to own every bodega in the neighborhood. They don't expect their children to take over the bodegas. They intend their kids to go to college to become professionals. For all these entrepreneurs, their journey is to make sure that their kids go to college.

These subtle shifts mean we need to build our political campaigns with more subtle variations. Technology is allowing us to use the ads that we develop in Colorado and adapt them for an audience in Arizona. The themes are similar, but the accents may shift. So we'll get a woman with a Venezuelan Spanish accent talking to a woman with a Puerto Rican accent, and we'll run that ad in Florida. These nuances are based on research underpinnings in given geographies. As much as I still believe that the main definition of Latinos is their country of origin, in terms of their politics, other factors are in play.

There's an assumption among some Republican political consultants that rising prosperity will allow them to peel away Latino support. I'm not so sure of that. Like American Jews, Latinos lean toward Democrats because they believe that Democrats care about people like them. That's why the issue of cancelling student debt is so important. It's a huge stumbling block for a family's progress to have to pay for college tuition. It represents another mortgage that will prevent children from doing better than their parents. I did focus-group studies for the Biden campaign among young people who graduated five or ten years ago. Canceling student debt was one of the most positive reasons for them to vote for Biden. If their debt was canceled, they could buy an apartment—something that would otherwise be impossible. Now that Republicans in the courts have stopped the Democrats' efforts to cancel a portion of student debt, let's remind young voters and their parents that we were close to providing some relief. Republicans stopped it.

The biggest difference in values, culturally and politically, between Latinos and white Americans is that we believe in the collective. Family isn't just Dad, Mom, kids, and a dog. Family includes a lot of people. It means you open your home, and you give to others. The notion that the nuclear family is the main object of advancement isn't real in our community.

Crime and gun safety are classic contests for Latino voters as we engage with these cultural and political battles with Republicans. Crime is a big issue for everybody—even me on the New York subway. Crime rates have gone down, but the news every day talks about random shootings. Latinos ask themselves, why do we allow any type of gun in anyone's hands? Our community understands that this is not a good policy. This isn't about what was important during the American Revolution. That's irrelevant now. If you talk to people, they'll tell you that you should have a gun if you own a bodega. If you need to protect something, that's a good reason. Because so much crime occurs in our community, people understand that you have to do something about it. The larger community is dismayed only when random shootings take place.

However, I can assure you that 90 percent of our community, like most of the country, rejects the idea that teachers should be armed as the only way to deter massacres in our schools. Gun control is an important motivator in getting Latinos out to vote precisely because we don't feel safe, and these extreme cases—these supposedly random events—are highlighted in the news everyday. Beto understood how to channel our grief into anger, which is the other side of grief. He could at least make us feel that there was an alternative outcome.

That's why Republicans will be under sustained pressure to do something in places, such as Texas and Georgia, that seemed to be their own strongholds. Their argument is that more guns are needed as the solution to gun violence. It makes no sense; it just creates a multiplying effect. Latinos will not buy it. In the past, Democratic leaders were reluctant to talk about guns, but that's changing. Texas may be more complicated, but in Georgia, it's unavoidable. Georgia is changing as more people move into the state from elsewhere.

In the last midterm cycle, we at Latino Victory worked with three candidates in Georgia who represented a good barometer of what's happening with Latinos across the country. Jason Esteves was a typical Puerto Rican, the son of migrants, born and raised in Georgia. He was the Google Image vision of a Puerto Rican Latino, big and tall with straight brown hair. The second, Phil Olaleye, had a Colombian dad and Nigerian immigrant mom and identified as Latino, even though he spoke a little less Spanish than the Puerto Rican candidate. He also proudly embraced his African American roots. The third candidate, Michelle Schreiner, had a background similar to that of my wife, Luz: mixed Latina (half Mexican, half Puerto Rican), born and raised in Georgia, working as a clinical psychologist with a doctorate behind her.

Each of the three Georgia candidates embraced a slightly different message, but there was a common denominator that works in our community: that government must continue to play an important role in our lives to help us prosper. It's a fallacy to think that this country gives you the freedom to be whatever you want to be. That happens only when there are mitigating factors, and government help is one of those important variables. There's absolutely nothing wrong with receiving government help to reach the other side of the bridge. This is an important message, and our community understands it. It's the counterargument to the idea that somehow, magically, an airplane ride from Puerto Rico gives you the freedom to "make it" in society. It was refreshing to hear all three candidates talk about this. Freddy Ferrer spoke about the same thing back when he was running for mayor twenty years ago. We need to give government the resources to help people, and many of our candidates—like Freddy—are prime examples of how that happens. It doesn't mean that you don't help yourself. But it does mean that we allow government to help you to get there.

The other through-line was that they were all clearly Latino. They never ran away from their identity. It was helpful for them in districts with large chunks of Latino voters. You need to be able to talk about your people and put your community in a larger context, where government and schools play an important role in our lives.

Of course, Latino culture is also more widely known and accepted—and that helps our Latino candidates. Back in the 1970s, when I arrived in New York, my white friends would tell me about their nanny or housekeeper who was Latino. I remember thinking, and sometimes saying, that that didn't sound cool to me. I came from a place where we weren't just the nannies and housekeepers but also the doctors and lawyers. My own nanny was Puerto Rican, but so was the lawyer who signed my divorce papers. Today, that familiarity and kinship are seeping through the culture.

At the same time, you can see the spread of the so-called replacement theory: that Latinos are here to replace white voters. That's what Trump amplified and represented. Trump gave everyone permission to say those racist thoughts out loud. Now those battles are being fought in parent associations and school boards, where they're selling replacement theory to otherwise normal, rational people.

We're still a society divided by our groupings. Many people don't like the idea that their group might be displaced by another. As minority groups continue to grow, there is an increased likelihood that a minority person might be elected to represent that district. At that point, in those places, our Latino identity can turn from a liability into an asset. That future—which is so unsettling for the people Trump represents—is already here.

CHAPTER 11

Rising Stars

Before they became famous, the rising stars of politics worked their way up. Barack Obama was a lowly state senator. AOC worked in a bar. Tish James was a lawyer in the New York State Assembly. If we want to increase diversity in our politics to reflect the diversity of our country, we need to look out for the next generation of rising stars—and support them as best we can, even if it means running against the Democratic establishment.

I first heard of Ricky Hurtado through a guy I met on Twitter. I have lots of Twitter friends, and this guy was relentless. I was intrigued. Ricky was running in North Carolina, trying to become the first Latino ever elected in the state legislature. I was very interested in the state in general and the way it was changing. Ricky called me one day and talked about his rural district, where Latinos—most of them, like Ricky, Mexican American—represented a little more than 10 percent of the voters.

My advice was that he shouldn't want to withhold the fact that he was Latino. After all, his name gives it away. But as a candidate, he just happens to be Latino. He needed to run a campaign about his identity as a rural guy who was born in that place: a teacher in the district where everyone sends their kids, where his wife is a teacher too. They were happy, hardworking people living happy, normal lives in rural North Carolina. They weren't looking for government jobs. He needed to build from his personal experience. Yes, when they met him, they would put his brown face together with his Spanish name. They knew who he was. But increasing diversity was not the message.

We agreed to support him at Latino Victory. However, it was clear to me that there was no way he would win without the support of the Democratic Party in the state. He was a first-time candidate, and even though the campaign was inexpensive, he needed party support. We helped him raise $20,000 toward the $50,000 he needed to run a decent campaign. But it wasn't enough on its own. So I flew to North Carolina to meet with the governor and the head of the state party. I had been a donor to the governor a couple of times, and we met over breakfast. I told him about this fantastic candidate who just happened to be Latino. They knew him. His experience was exactly the same as that of the people in his district, but he had a Spanish name and a brown face. For people who were really committed to diversity in their state, this was their chance to elect the first-ever Latino, with the support of the governor and the Democratic Party. The governor agreed.

Ricky is a regular guy with progressive attitudes, but he doesn't wear his progressive politics on his sleeve. That's not how you get elected in his district. However, you can talk about Medicare for All, where anyone can buy into the Medicare system, no matter how old they are, because all his neighbors are struggling with health care. His white neighbors aren't affluent people. They all struggle with the cost of prescriptions and doctors. Ricky speaks their language. If you transported him to New York, he would be close to Alexandria Ocasio-Cortez in terms of his own thinking about what needs to change. But in North Carolina, he's just a regular guy who wants to do good for his neighbors. He may be to the left of most of them, but he has the same life experiences and he paid his dues by being a good teacher to their kids. He didn't have a network of people who could raise money for him or a network of connected officials who saw him as one of their own.

Ricky won the election, making history in North Carolina. The second time around, he lost, running against the same opponent. Now he has the support of his party and can raise his own money. Hopefully, he will run again! But that first contest was a steep hill to climb.

The challenge for those of us who want to increase diversity among our elected officials is how to nationalize a race like that. Other Latino candidates and supporters want to know that there's someone like Ricky in North Carolina. It becomes important to know that they're part of a large network of up-and-coming Latino elected officials. They're part of building the bench of Latino rising stars.

Ricky won, in part, by gaining the support of the 10 percent of voters in his district who are Latinos. You have to start with your base. Other candidates don't embrace that, at their peril. I once worked with a perfect Latina candidate in Massachusetts. She was intelligent, totally bilingual, and very engaging. However, her team was concerned about campaigning too heavily in the Latino community—even though she was running in a district that was 30 percent Latino. I kept telling her to worry about that 30 percent. She was running against a white woman who was ideologically identical to her. So her advantage was that she could win the overwhelming support of Latino voters; they would vote for her before they would vote for a white woman with similar ideas. When they met her, they could talk to her in Spanish or English and like her for who she was. When they met her rival, they couldn't talk to her like that. Our candidate was a member of the family.

Instead, she surrounded herself with consultants who convinced her that she should focus on winning the white voters. I kept telling them that yes, she could do that. But the white voters already had a white woman. Why not lean into what sets you apart?

My candidate struggled with her campaign. I recruited a busload of Dominican volunteers to support her because she was of Dominican origin. They knocked on doors, but they knew she was in trouble. It was more difficult and costly to get white votes than Latino votes. She lost her contest.

If you want to win, you need to create a formula that starts with getting as many votes from your own group as possible. Then figure out how many votes you need from the other groups. With Freddy, we knew we needed to overperform with Latinos (which we did) and get 20 percent of the white vote. We failed to do that, and we lost.

Five years ago, I met a young attorney in Georgia who took the winning approach. I was campaigning for another candidate, knocking on doors in a Latino neighborhood. People are surprised when I say that I want to knock on doors, but it's true. I want to talk to people and meet them. One of the people who was also knocking on doors was Deborah Gonzalez, who wanted to be district attorney in her small town of Athens. She had no real organization, but she had a lot of heart and smarts.

Deborah was fully bilingual and fully engaged. She didn't mind knocking on doors herself, but she knew that her own politics were to the left of her district. "So let's figure out what your district can live with in terms of criminal justice," I said. "We don't have to talk about it if we don't want to. Let's talk about the things you have in common with your constituents."

First, she needed money: $30,000 to run a successful campaign. I asked her how much money she could raise, and she told me she could lend the campaign $1,000 and perhaps raise another $4,000 from friends. It took only one attempt to raise the other $25,000 for her. We nationalized her race, introducing her as the first Puerto Rican woman district attorney in the country, and we raised the money with one virtual fundraiser. We emailed twenty Puerto Rican friends across the country saying, "We have an opportunity to elect a DA to a small town. We have to start somewhere, and she's Puerto Rican. Very smart and very progressive. Probably too progressive for the people she wants to represent, but someone who will make us proud."

In three hours, we raised the money. The email was passed around to other Puerto Ricans, who were all eager to see a candidate like Deborah succeed.

You wouldn't know from her appearance that she's Puerto Rican. Deborah is fair-skinned, and her hair is blondish. But when she speaks Spanish, with no accent, you know that she is Puerto Rican. Of course, her name gives her away. But she ran as Deborah for Georgia. She was never shy about being who she was, but we didn't shout about her being called Gonzalez. She was raised in the community and worked there. Her neighbors knew her, even though she was of different origins. They all shared the same experiences. Nobody was parachuted in.

———

THIS IS HOW FOX NEWS POISONS PEOPLE, BY SPREADING RACIST propaganda that Latinos and Blacks are different and threatening. It feeds this poison on a twenty-four-hour drip. It tells people that Latinos are coming across the border to rape and kill their kids. So that's what people think. Without Fox, and other right-wing media just like it, our politics would be so different. We might have 20 percent of Americans who think like that, but not the 35 percent who say they do. That makes a difference. In reality, people are for the most part good. They like their neighbors, even if their families come from some other place.

It's a strange political calculation for Republicans. Employers cannot make money because there aren't enough workers in this economy. Normally immigration would fill the gap. In Puerto Rico, after Hurricane Maria, we worked with a coalition of organizations, led by the Hispanic Federation, to rebuild the coffee industry. But there's nobody to pick the coffee, and the government is trying to figure out whether we can import people from Haiti or Mexico. I have friends who own small restaurants, and they cannot find people to hire. They cannot open for breakfast in my neighborhood. Some of them struggle to open at lunch. If Monday is their slowest day, they close the entire restaurant on Mondays because they cannot find enough people.

Still, it's an easy political argument for Republicans to make to a large white population who cannot achieve their aspirations as their parents did. Rather than talking about the real economic translocation of a changing economy—and rather than getting into the difficult ways of solving that—it's so much easier to say, "That motherfucker took your job." In reality, he or she didn't take your job. In fact, most Americans believe that immigrants take the jobs they don't want. They will never go pick vegetables in a hot field for hours on end or take care of our elderly population. Latinos do that work because they just hope their kids will go to a better school and have a different life.

Immigration is not a simple issue for Democrats, who often mistakenly assume that Latinos just want more immigration. What they want is a more humane approach to immigration. You can see this all the time when you watch Univision or Telemundo. They pick people to interview in border towns, where it cannot be easy to live. They see people running through their backyard or camping in their plaza. Who wouldn't be a little freaked out if they saw people coming through their driveway? New York is living some of that now, and many are freaking out there too. Invariably, when those people are interviewed, they say we need a humane solution, that this cannot continue. People realize that if you walked hundreds of miles with little kids to make it to the border after traveling another eight hundred miles on buses and trains, there's something very wrong in your country of origin. What I have seen over and over again is that people want this issue solved so that we can have an orderly transition to move people. Except for extremists on the other side of Trump, people understand that those who are living here should get the papers they need so they can emerge from the shadows. They are already productive members of society. I have never met one Latino who says, "Send them back on a plane."

———

NOBODY THOUGHT GREG CASAR COULD WIN HIS RACE FOR A NEW congressional district in Texas. The Republican Texas legislature was gerrymandering the state and didn't know what do with San Antonio and Austin, so it connected them along the expressway to create the only new Democratic district in the weirdest possible shape. Greg is like Ricky and Deborah: he has worked in the community. He speaks Spanish as well as English, which is very important if you want to attract Latino voters. Half of his family is in Mexico, and the other half is in Texas. He even has family members who go back and forth across the border. So he could switch languages to deliver the same message to all kinds of voters.

However, Greg is ideologically a socialist, to the left of AOC. And he was running against another Latino who had been elected to the legislature for a decade or more. It helped that he had a relatively short record in office as a former Austin city council member. It's easier when your record is what comes out of your mouth rather than the difficult votes you've cast in the statehouse. But his real strength was his economic message. He spoke about economic issues in ways that connected with people. He spoke about how the minimum wage should be $15 so people wouldn't need two jobs to make ends meet. He talked about subsidized housing. That allowed him to win a chunk of progressive Austin, along with the heavily Latino areas of San Antonio. He was an anomaly in Texas, and his progressive politics led to an endorsement by Bernie Sanders. That helped him in Austin and didn't take away from his Latino support in San Antonio. He won decisively in his primary contest without the need for a runoff.

Greg couldn't have won in Florida with that kind of socialist background among Latino voters of Venezuelan or Cuban origin. You need to know your market. He could win in New York, and maybe in Los Angeles. But among an immigrant community that fled socialism at home? No way.

Republicans understand this dynamic in more conservative places such as Texas, Florida, and Georgia. That's why they find Latino candidates who also speak the language—and why they are elected by Latinos. They argue that we're not children, that we don't need government help that costs trillions of dollars. They claim that the money is stolen, that Democrats spend money in our communities, but we remain poor. And that the only way to prosper is to work hard.

All of that is perfectly acceptable messaging in Spanish. So we have to explain that sometimes we still don't have the money to pay for tuition. There's nothing wrong with government helping with that. After all, that's what taxes are for: to help our kids get an education that we couldn't otherwise afford. Government help isn't demeaning. It should be uplifting. A handout is the government's responsibility to give you a hand whenever you need a hand. As a single mother, before we married, my wife relied on food stamps so she could complete her PhD.

Still, Republicans have wised up to the same trends among Latino voters, and their bar is much lower. Democrats need the majority of the Latino vote to win elections, but that's not the case for Republicans. They need from one-quarter to one-third of the vote. So when you look at the states that performed well for Democrats in the 2022 midterms, it was places—such as Pennsylvania—where we got 70 percent of the Latino vote instead of 66 percent. We did the same in Georgia. It's the difference between electing a Republican or a Democrat as a US senator. We're working day and night to increase the number of Latinos going out to vote so that we can drive our numbers up by two, three, or four points.

That's a precarious position to be in, especially when Democrats have taken that vote for granted for a long time. Democrats used to have enough working-class white votes, along with Black votes, to put us over the top. Latinos were icing on the cake. Now that coalition has broken apart, Latinos are much more important. We're in play, and Democrats need to work hard for minuscule percentages in some places. That's why it often feels like Democrats are playing catch-up: we didn't lay the foundations for the Latino vote so that we could behave politically like the African American vote. Republicans can spend much less, and their work is much easier, because the goal is so much lower. In Georgia, for instance, we identified 126,000 Spanish surnames on voter rolls, but 70 percent of them turned out to be incorrect. We have not invested in creating an infrastructure, such as good voter lists. We have to invest so much more to increase our percentage of the pie by marginal amounts, because we failed to invest over the years. In New York, it's different because we have built the infrastructure. That means when you get a list of Latino voters in New York, 80 percent of the names are good.

The variety of Latino identities also makes the challenge more complex and costly. In Pennsylvania, we could target Puerto Rican areas, with a few Dominican enclaves, so it was a Caribbean message that cut through. The Puerto Rican community there is much older, with real roots in the communities. But in Georgia, we were speaking to Mexican Americans, with only small numbers of Puerto Ricans. There have been Mexicans in Georgia for a long time, but many never became citizens, and the newer Mexican American citizens aren't yet involved in politics. The messaging across just these two battleground states requires real thinking and real work. There are very few campaigns that are willing to do that, not least because it involves putting money into this work.

The 2022 midterms underscored the challenges—not just for Democrats but also for Republicans. There were three tests for whether the Republicans could build a Latino wave, and they failed most of them, according to analysis by Equis Research, which specializes in studying Latino engagement. Republicans won over more Latino voters in Florida, but only because of higher turnout—not because Latinos switched parties. They failed to improve on Trump's support in Nevada and Arizona. And they failed to win any districts in south Texas that had voted for President Biden. Texas Governor Greg Abbott promised to win half the Latino vote in south Texas, but he didn't improve on Trump's performance in the Rio Grande Valley in 2022. These Republican failures among Latinos help explain why Republicans underperformed in key races across the country.

However, it's worth understanding why Republicans continue to gain in their share of the Latino vote in Florida. Democrats have steadily lost support among Latino voters in Florida since President Obama's reelection campaign in 2012, to the point that our candidates for senator and governor were as much as 20 points behind his performance. Only Hillary Clinton in 2016 broke the trend, and she outperformed the Democratic candidate for the Senate that year by 20 points herself. Florida's Republicans have invested consistently in their Latino outreach to the extent that Governor Ron DeSantis lost the Latino vote in his first election and won it the second time around. The DeSantis team never stopped campaigning for Latino voters, and after four years, the results were clear. The Trump team did something similar during their four years in power. Investment in Latino outreach works, no matter which party spends the time and money to do so.

On the other hand, Republicans cannot escape their deep internal conflicts about Latinos and immigration in particular. For all their gains among Venezuelans in Florida, Republicans still find a way to treat Venezuelans like political footballs rather than human beings. When Ron DeSantis flies dozens of Venezuelan migrants to Martha's Vineyard, he might generate all the headlines he wants in the Trump-aligned media. But it's hard to see how Venezuelan Americans think this is a good idea for people like them, who are escaping the misery in their country of origin. Especially when the migrants were misled about where they were going and why. Republicans might not need many Latino voters to build their winning coalition, but they're already in danger of taking their Latino voters for granted.

By far the top issues for Latino voters are economic ones: inflation, jobs, and wages. However, beneath the headline issues, there are significant differences between Latino men and Latina women. For women, abortion and guns rank as highly as inflation and higher than jobs. Immigration reform ranks far down the list, as important as voting rights and foreign policy. Why are voters aligned with Democrats? The biggest reasons are to protect Social Security and Medicare, abortion rights, the environment, and our democracy. These may be good reasons to vote, but they don't align with the top economic issues for Latino voters. Until Democrats can improve their appeal in relation to the economy, the Latino vote will remain vulnerable.

In the meantime, Latino voters are already changing the face of Congress, sending more Latino officials to Washington than ever before. In the 2022 midterms, Democrats elected nine new Latinos from nine different states, while Republicans elected five Latinos. The contrast between them was hard to miss. Among the Democrats were Greg Casar from Texas and Maxwell Alejandro Frost from Orlando,

Florida, the youngest member of Congress at just twenty-six years old. Among the Republicans were Anna Paulina Luna from Florida, who only recently decided to identify as Latina, and George Santos from Long Island, New York, a Brazilian American serial fabulist whose real name is not even George Santos. He was later indicted on multiple fraud charges and expelled from Congress—only the sixth member to suffer that fate in congressional history.

———

LETITIA JAMES IS MY KIND OF LEADER. I WAS INTRIGUED BY THE fact that she won her seat on the New York City Council as a candidate of the Working Families Party after losing her spot in the Democratic primary. I met her through my business partner Eddy Castell, who's from Brooklyn, like Tish. I was fascinated by her. She was a bit out there in terms of her politics, to the left, as I am. But there was also a lot of realism in the positions she took and engaged with. She was running for public advocate in 2013, and she asked us to manage her campaign. Her campaign didn't have two pennies to rub together. We were running against a self-funded candidate from a rich family and another candidate with a Spanish name through marriage—which led a chunk of Latino voters to incorrectly assume that she was Hispanic. So we depended on media coverage and on Tish's ability to be great at the only public debate of the campaign. She won, and we literally had no money to spend on a victory party.

When the position of New York state attorney general opened up after Eric Schneiderman resigned in disgrace, Tish said she was interested. We had just seventy-two hours to decide, so I spent some time negotiating with Governor Andrew Cuomo for them to be on the same ticket. It wasn't an easy position for Tish or me. But I live in the real world. I had seen the polls. Andrew Cuomo drew more support from African Americans than Tish herself. Of course, this was all before Cuomo himself resigned in disgrace. But people were saying that Tish couldn't support Cuomo because of his centrist politics. She was the candidate of the left-wing Working Families Party. However, the alternative was Cynthia Nixon, who played Miranda in *Sex and the City*. She was a famous actor but had no chance of defeating Cuomo.

So Tish joined forces with Cuomo, but I knew whom we were electing. She isn't the kind of person that you help elect and then she's in your pocket for the rest of your life. That's not Tish James. So when the Cuomo sex allegations emerged and Tish was tasked with the investigation, she did the right thing. She could have been governor herself at that point if she had wanted to run. But her heart wasn't in it.

She would have been a stronger governor than Kathy Hochul, who succeeded Cuomo. Hochul almost lost her election in 2022, and that wouldn't have happened with Tish James as the candidate. Tish has a set of principles. She's one of eight children, the daughter of a school janitor in Brooklyn. Her life was forged in reality. That's the backbone of who she is. There's not a ton of elasticity in her beliefs. She doesn't bend because of budget items. She runs on real issues, and she has real positions on those issues. She's also an inspirational speaker who can move whole rooms full of people.

She represents what Democrats need in their rising stars: someone who knows who she is and doesn't run on poll numbers.

———

IT ISN'T EASY FIGURING OUT WHO MIGHT BE THE FIRST LATINO OR Latina president of the United States. My guess is that it will be someone like one of the Castro brothers, Julian or Joaquin, from

San Antonio, Texas. They're from a huge electoral state with lots of Latinos, giving them a solid foundation of votes. They're well known and good communicators, and they have done their homework. Their politics are right, which is important in winning the Democratic nomination while not alienating the center.

We need to unite the ideological factions of the party as well as different minority identities. Often these challenges overlap. Barack Obama convinced African Americans to set aside their differences. As Latinos, we have more ideological and cultural differences, and we have to move beyond them all. When I ran Freddy Ferrer's mayoral campaign, Latinos were around 20 percent of the city's population but just 12 or 13 percent of the vote. There were too many young people and too many noncitizens. For us to get to the magic 40 percent of the vote to win the primary, we needed solid African American support, an overperformance by Latinos, and a good 20 percent of the white vote. We surpassed our goals with African Americans and Latinos, but we couldn't carry the white votes. Freddy was an instance of a left-of-center candidate who convinced minority voters to come together despite their differences. We need someone like that at the presidential level. Indeed, we need someone who can convince right-of-center Latinos to join the broader coalition.

A Latina may have a better chance of winning the Latino vote. There are more women than men who vote in our community. They are also on the right side of issues such as abortion rights and gun control. That means someone like Rochelle Garza can emerge as a serious contender. Rochelle is young, smart, and hardworking. She won the Democratic primary for Texas attorney general with the massive support of Latinos. But the Democratic establishment in her state and throughout the country did not invest in her race against the now-impeached Texas attorney general Ken Paxton. We believed in her so much that Lin-Manuel went to Texas and campaigned for her. Mark my words: Rochelle is going places. She is the future of the Democratic Party.

The first Latino president will not be a Republican, in my view. A Republican candidate could not convince Latinos to set aside their differences or Republicans to set aside their prejudice. It takes thirty seconds to look at the Republican Party platform before you start a real discussion with a Latino candidate on that side. How can they defend this ideology while still believing in multiculturalism? They belong to a different kind of party, and in its current form, we're not welcome.

I hope to be alive to see it happen. I'm sure there's a young person out there who will become our first Latinx president. They may be in some city council or state legislature. We all saw how Obama ascended to victory from a lowly perch in Illinois. He was propelled by young people who were committed to getting out the vote. In our family, as in so many others, it was our children who pushed us. In every other election, they participated in the political process because I pushed them to do so. They had no choice. But when it came to that election, it was different. My son was very excited about Obama. My daughter was very excited about Hillary Clinton.

Our first Latino president will change this country. She or he will be the perfect response to Donald Trump and the ugliness he has unleashed. We will change the course of history, just as we have already changed the course of this country. Because we are relentless.

CHAPTER 12

The End

THAT WAS A LIFE WELL LIVED. NOW IT'S TIME, IN THIS FINAL chapter, to plan my funeral. I do this in part because I'm a control freak but also because I want to share with my family and friends my vision (as morbid as it sounds) of what I want for my last goodbye to the many people I love. I don't know if you get to experience what's going on in the world after you die. I don't know if you're somewhere else, and you know what's happening but just don't get to watch it. Whatever it is we experience in death, if my family and friends follow this recipe, it won't matter where I am because my last wishes will have been implemented.

Can I have a celebration at the magnificent United Palace theater in Washington Heights? Can a simple coffin, painted by neighborhood graffiti artists, with the casket closed, be standing in the lobby? I would like my body to wear a linen guayabera. Since I will be cremated, beautiful simplicity seems an appropriate last look.

Before the doors open to whoever wants to come to my last goodbye in the United Palace lobby, I would like some time alone with my family. I don't care if they sing, stare at each other, pray, or simply talk. I want them all together so they can continue to be together even when I'm physically gone. I worry myself sick that because I spend so much of my time trying to be the glue for a family separated by geography and busy lives, they'll drift apart when I'm no longer present. I need Luz, Cita and Luis, Lin-Manuel and Vanessa, and Miguel and Landa. I could not have gone through life without them. They give me something to worry about, something to love, something to live for. I need my grandchildren. I don't know how old they will be (hopefully very old!) when I die, but they are becoming terrific humans. My grandchildren are following their own very unique paths: from Frankie and Sebastián's very different but quirky and big personalities to Hunter's thoughtful approach to life; from Luisito's fun manner and Alejandro's serious demeanor to D. Javier's theatrical exuberance. I also want to make sure my brother, Elvin, and my sister, Yamilla, are there. After fifty years of living apart, separated by 1,614 miles, they are present in my daily experience of life. And of course their families—Rosita, Kevin, Camila, and Daniela. In this last family gathering with me, let's make sure my sister-in-law, Jackie Bilotta, and her wonderful husband, Bob, are there.

I want to spend some time with both my family and my family members by choice. They should all be there, starting with Michael Stolper, my New York brother. I turn to him in my hour of need and love spending time with him and the family he brought into my life—Melissa, Rianna, my godson Jack, and Carlos. Lorraine Cortés-Vázquez is my New York sister. She makes me laugh and always has good insights. JJ—John Antonio James—dedicated a chunk of his professional life to directing a documentary movie about me. How sweet is that? And I know he worries about me and my well-being. I love Owen Panettieri and Sara Miller as if they were my kids. They have had my back for decades. Then there is Roberto, my business partner, or my other wife, as Luz used to call him. John Gutierrez and Niria Leyva-Gutierrez are good, smart, and loyal people who have been a special part of my life since 1990. Nathalie Rayes protects me like a hawk and has brought so much joy to my life. I want to make sure Maria Calle, our faithful housekeeper and friend, is there. For decades, she has taken care of so many of us. Also with us should be David Ocasio, my trainer, and George Diaz, who have taken care of my body (as it ages) and my hair (thank God I have some) for decades.

Is it possible to legislate that all these wonderful people continue to meet, at least once a year, to celebrate their relationship with me and among themselves? My funeral should be the first of these annual reunions.

But I digress. Back to my funeral details.

After this intimate moment, let people come into the theater. And let the celebration begin! "Amanecer Borincano" by Alberto Carrión should start the playlist. Lin-Manuel can take the lead in putting the playlist together. He gave me many mixtapes for Father's Day when he had no money, and they were the most cherished gifts I got from him.

Some song requests: "Soy de Una Raza Pura" by Lucecita Benítez; "Ojalá que Llueva Café" by Juan Luis Guerra; "How Far I'll Go," "Dos Oruguitas," "Paciencia y Fé," "Almost Like Praying,"

"One More Time," and "Yorktown" by Lin-Manuel; "Perla Marina" from Haciendo Punto en Otro Son; "I Believe in You and Me" by Whitney Houston; "Tonight" from *West Side Story*; "I'll Never Say No" from *The Unsinkable Molly Brown*; and "Corner of the Sky" from *Pippin*. I believe my family can brainstorm a little to complete my playlist.

Then let's go into the theater and a short concert can begin. I know it can take a lot of work to put a band and a chorus together and for them to learn the concert music. Maybe I'll ask the musical geniuses Alex Lacamoire and Tommy Kail to be in charge. They know enough musicians and singers to pull it all together. It doesn't have to be the Philharmonic; it just needs to be beautiful. I know that if Alex and Tommy are in charge, it will be fantastic. Let's put a chorus together: some nice voices harmonizing for a last goodbye. I can close my eyes and see the beautiful faces and angelic voices of Lin-Manuel's friends at his wedding or the glorious students from the school of music in Puerto Rico who played for Cita's wedding. If we can do it for weddings, we can surely do it for my funeral too.

In between songs, several people must talk. Let's start with "Preciosa" by Rafael Hernández. I wish Luz would welcome everyone afterward. I know she is a tough lady and can say a couple of things about me. I was twenty-four when I started my journey with her. No one knows me better. No one will miss me more than she will. Believe me, I know she loves it when I go on trips or leave her alone in the house to enjoy her shows and puzzles without reminding her that she is wasting valuable time. She will even miss my constant reminders to set a goal for the next hour, the next day, and the rest of our lives. But this time, my trip will be for the rest of her life. She'll be fine! I'll miss her until we meet again somewhere else.

For the next song—before Nathalie Rayes and Frankie Miranda talk about my work, my love of politics, and my passion for community—I need Lin-Manuel to pick a *Hamilton* song. Whether I die tomorrow or two decades from now, *Hamilton* changed our lives. First, it provided Lin-Manuel, and all of us, with a big stage from which we could highlight our causes and passions. It also changed our fortunes from a middle-class family to one with additional resources to support our community and political work. Frankie and Nathalie are young enough to be around for a while. Frankie has been entrusted with one of my most important legacies—the Hispanic Federation—and Nathalie has supported my political work for Latinos nationwide.

Then it will be time for Michael and Roberto to speak about what it was like to soportarme—to put up with me—by choice. We had a very long journey together, and they can highlight whatever they want. Hopefully Roberto can touch on our work life. We waged many battles side by side. We assembled a courageous and smart army with great leaders—Eddy Castell, Catherine Torres, John Emrick, Melissa Mark-Viverito, Tony Reyes. Michael can speak about our army of friends. I have never been very good at separating work from life. Work is life, and life is family. If there are no boundaries, you accomplish more.

When Lin-Manuel's companies became a reality, we little by little assembled another fun and smart army that made deals happen through philanthropy and entertainment. Sara can go onstage and share with everyone some of the magic that we were able to make with Lin-Manuel at the helm. She can talk about how everything we did had integrity and love as our north stars. I am sure she will talk about how my son's agent John Buzzetti, lawyer Nancy Rose, and agent Brian Liebman led the protection squad with a great sense of humor and humanity and learned that equity and inclusion make a room shine more brightly. Lin-Manuel's 5000 Broadway team was terrific. Even though it was small, our impact was gigantic.

Lin-Manuel will close this procession of friends and music. I wish it could go on forever, but short and sweet makes a better and bigger impression. And then it will be time to put together the trip to leave some of my ashes in those places that served as beautiful sets for my life: Venice, Vega Alta, Montauk, and an urn at my resting place in New York.

As I close this book of my life, I am filled with joy. I am finishing this last chapter as I fly home with Luz, Sara, and Hugo Wehe—the most recent addition to my squad of very special people—after receiving an Icon Award from Latinx House in Aspen, Colorado. There I told a room full of people that the work must continue on behalf of our community and our country. The celebrations were still going when I left to rush home because today is the eighteenth birthday of my oldest grandson, Luisito.

———

Is it possible to encapsulate a life in a paragraph? Let's try.

The best thing I did in my life was migrating to New York City. That act was impulsive but intentional. When I was about to close that chapter and return to Puerto Rico, I engaged in another impulsive but intentional act: marrying Luz and becoming an instant dad, a role that expanded when we welcomed Lin-Manuel and Miguel into our lives. We moved to Upper Manhattan, allowing my family to become champions of our turf in New York City—and champions of the largest community of neighbors: Latinos. My passion for service led me to the noblest of careers—to serve, to advocate, and to build. There wasn't an area I did not venture into—government, the independent sector, philanthropy, private industry. As Paul Anka wrote in his English lyrics of a French song, "I did it my way."

It has been a great life, and my greatest privilege has been to share it with so many gente linda y luchadora.

Acknowledgments

How do you begin to thank those whom you know—and those you don't—who helped shape who you are, informed your thinking, and provided support that helped you move forward? Do you stop with those who've impacted you personally, or do you also include those who've inspired loved ones and, in turn, made a difference in your life? Do you focus only on those who are alive? These questions are so nuanced that this is the last chapter I wrote after the book itself was finished. I could write a long acknowledgments chapter because I love so many people, but I will narrow my scope. Here is my attempt to thank some of the many people who've made a difference, whether they've been in my life for a short time or decades but whose presence has forever changed who I am:

No other group of people has impacted my life more than my kids (Cita, Lin-Manuel, and Miguel), my life partner (Luz), my parents (Eva and Güisin), my surrogate mother, Mundi, my brother, Elvin, and my sister, Yamilla. They constantly feed me love, ideas, energy to do things, problems to resolve, or resolutions to problems. I have no clue who I'd be without them.

I have been lucky that Cita, Lin-Manuel, and my brother Elvin found partners—Luis Crespo, Vanessa Nadal, and Rosa Arroyo—who complete them and bring joy to my life.

My grandchildren, Hunter, Luisito, Alejandro, Dylan Javier, Sebastián, and Francisco, whose wit, smartness, and talents keep me young and hopeful for the future.

Forever grateful to Mamá Suncha (Asunción Vega), Titi Juanita, and Titi Sarita (Juanita and Sara Concepción) and Luz's parents (Pedro and Mimi Towns), all deceased, who lent us the money for our house down payment in Upper Manhattan. Without them, so much of our family life, philanthropy, and advocacy would have taken another form, and there probably would not have been a musical called *In the Heights*!

My music teacher Raquel Rodriguez, who—in choreographing "Do-Re-Mi" from *The Sound of Music*—sparked my love of theater and music, something that has never left me all these years later. My uncles Ernesto and Rodolfo Concepción and my aunt Elsie Moreau nurtured that love and turned it into a life passion.

Five people who changed the trajectory of my life: Bernie Kalinkowitz and my aunt Abigail Diaz de Concepción, who introduced New York City as the destination of my life; Norma Stanton, who made NYC welcoming and familiar; Lou Cassotta, who helped me process my life with tools to use in the future; and Esmeralda Diaz Santiago, who—when I was ready to go back to Puerto Rico—asked me, "Do you want to go back when you are falling in love with Luz?"

There was a group of students who became my support group during my tough, early years in NYC. Nydia Velázquez became my sister, providing comfort during my divorce at twenty years old. Jeannette Roselló and Lillian Pérez were my "angelitos," helping me navigate language and social expectations. Also, Anita Soto and Jorge Colberg (both deceased) were always there for me when I needed them.

Aspira of New York and Asociación Comunal de Dominicanos Progresistas (ACDP) were organizational models in my life for advocacy, organizing, and community change. The people I met in those institutions, like María Irizarry, Guillermo and Evelyn Linares, Ernesto Loperena, and Felicidad and Viterbo Peguero, changed who I was, and those institutions served as laboratories where I learned the skills I needed to develop the Hispanic Federation and my passion for nonprofits as a force for social change.

Jack Olivero, Roberto Ramírez, Guillermo Linares, former mayor Ed Koch, and Fernando Ferrer turned me to politics because of its transformative impact.

The handful of people who were part of the original team to develop the Hispanic Federation are forever in my heart: Nereida Andino, John Gutierrez, Doris Peña, Mariano Gúzman, Tony Reyes, Carlos Santiago, and Michael Stolper. Its subsequent leaders—Lorraine Cortés-Vázquez, Lillian Rodriguez Lopez, José Calderón, and Frankie Miranda—are the reason why, thirty-four years later, the institution continues to thrive.

The overlapping of heroes and heroines through my life is remarkable. When I meet someone who touches my heart (and is smart), I carry them forever: Stan Brezenoff and Diane Coffey during the Koch administration; Terry Baker and the late Anthony Alvarado at the Board of Education; Carol Morning, who lured me to the National Action Council for Minorities in Engineering; and Raulito Alarcón, who has been my friend since he hired me at Mega in 1989.

My partners at MirRam Group—Roberto Ramírez, Catherine Torres, Eduardo Castell, John Emrick, and my daughter, Cita— who have been able to create and foster a for-profit with a soul and mission that will outlive me.

I love John James and his family, not only because he is a loving soul but also because he was the first to see my life story as one worth sharing and created *Siempre, Luis.*

The Sunshine team, led by Kenny Sunshine, has been with us from day one: Blake Ross and Jessica Berger, Charlie Guadano (whom we stole for our team), Jason Lee and Alex Cutler. They help us navigate the complicated world of PR and communications.

My friends and neighbors at Global Strategy Group: Jef Pollock, Jon Silvan, Jeff Plant and Marc Litvinoff, who are always there when I need them. We have fought many political battles side by side.

There are some good people I have picked along the way, some dating back over thirty years: Sara Elisa Miller, who gives me more fun work than anyone else in my life; Owen Panettieri, a constant in my life who cares deeply and supports our family; Niria Leyva-Gutierrez, who has become a key player personally and professionally; Javier Gómez, who works 24/7; John Buzzetti and Nancy Rose, whose advice is valued to no end; Jill Furman, Jeffrey Seller, Kevin McCollum and Sandy Jacobs, whose support and belief in my son Lin-Manuel changed my life as well; Carrie Catapano, whose dedication and influence helped in shaping Miguel's trajectory; Nathalie Rayes, who protects me and has been a partner in developing Latino Victory and the Hispanic Federation; and Hugo Wehe, who entered my life five years ago and, though he is young enough to be my grandson, has become a trusted adviser.

Finally, this book would never have happened without the constant work and nudging of Whitney Williams and her team. She found my collaborator, Richard Wolffe, who has become a beacon in the writing of *Relentless*; my lawyer, Bob Barnett; and our publisher, Hachette, and she has shepherded this entire process with thoughtfulness and finesse.

Index